Off The Record
Things A Therapist Won't Say

Carolyn Miller, LCSW

Dedication

This book is dedicated to the wonderfully resilient humans I've had the privilege of walking alongside on their journeys. Your stories, your laughter, even your tears, have taught me more than any textbook ever could. This book is a testament to your strength, your courage, and your unwavering spirit. And to my own family, Jimmy, Ayden, and Caleb - who tolerate my endless musings on the human condition with remarkable grace. Thank you for reminding me that even therapists need therapy.

Preface

So, you're holding this book. Maybe you picked it up because you're curious about therapy. Perhaps you're navigating a particularly rough patch in life and are looking for some insight (or maybe just a good laugh). Whatever your reason, welcome! I wrote this book because I believe that the human experience, even in its messiest moments, is both fascinating and hilarious. My years as a therapist have provided me with a front-row seat to the rollercoaster of emotions, the triumphs and the failures, the sheer absurdity of it all.

This isn't a self-help manual with a list of five easy steps to a perfect life (sorry, no magic wand here). Instead, it's a peek behind the curtain of a therapist's office. It's a collection of stories – lightly fictionalized, naturally, to protect the identities of my very real and very interesting clients – that offer a glimpse into the struggles, anxieties, and joys that bind us together. Think of it as a friendly chat, a shared journey through the tangled landscape of the human heart, where we'll explore everything from the emotional fallout of a messy divorce to the surprisingly common anxiety about doing laundry.

I've tried to weave humor throughout, because let's face it, sometimes laughter is the best medicine (and sometimes the only medicine we can stomach when facing life's inevitable curveballs). But don't mistake the humor for a lack of seriousness. The issues we'll explore are real, challenging, and often deeply painful. The goal is to offer empathy, understanding, and perhaps a new perspective, all within a framework that's both accessible and engaging. So grab a cup of coffee, tea (or a glass of wine, no judgment here), settle in, and let's explore the wonderfully messy, sometimes chaotic, and ultimately hilarious world of human experience together.

Introduction

Life. It's a beautiful, messy, often chaotic ride, isn't it? One minute you're soaring high on a wave of happiness, the next you're face-planting into a pile of anxieties, responsibilities, and the ever-present existential dread of whether you've actually put enough SPF on. As a therapist, I've witnessed this emotional roller coaster countless times, and let me tell you, it's a wild ride with unexpected twists and turns you never see coming.

This book isn't about providing easy fixes or quick solutions. There's no magic formula to erase stress, or a secret code to unlock ultimate happiness. Life doesn't work that way, and frankly, if it did, I'd be writing a different kind of book. Instead, this book is an exploration of the common ground we all share in the complexities of the human experience. It's about those moments where we feel utterly lost, completely overwhelmed, and maybe just a little bit ridiculous.

This book is about things a therapist *won't* tell you. Things we are thinking while working with you, things we wish we can say but know we shouldn't. We'll dive into familiar territory, exploring the trials and tribulations of relationships, the pressures of work, the challenges of parenting, and the everyday anxieties that can feel surprisingly monumental. We'll tackle tough topics with a sense of humor, because sometimes a good laugh is the best way to acknowledge the absurdity of it all and find the strength to keep going. This offers a glimpse into the realities of life and the struggles we all face. And the things a therapist *won't say* ....but wishes she could!

1. Divorce Your Spouse

Your therapist won't tell you divorce your spouse (but she *really* wants to).

She will listen to the struggles, the frustration, the arguments, the poor communication (none of which, by the way, mean you should in fact get divorced). But more than that, she will observe the impact all of this has on you. Your therapist's main priority is you and your healthcare. If they work with you over a period of time, see you taking suggestions well, implementing healthy changes and making efforts on your own to improve the state of your marriage, yet your marriage is still harmful to you, they won't tell you to divorce your spouse. But she most certainly will be thinking about it.

Some of the most compelling arguments against divorce are those surrounding faith beliefs, and child rearing. "God doesn't like divorce, it goes against my faith to 'give up' on my marriage." Sometimes coupled with "I don't want my children to grow up in a broken home. I want to set a good example for my child." Or simply "I don't believe in divorce, it goes against my values." These arguments against divorce are important, compelling, and full of truth. However, none of them honor the fact that sometimes a marriage can be so unhealthy, it is detrimental to a family. God doesn't like an unhealthy marriage anymore than He likes divorce. God values the individual in the marriage more than the constitution of marriage as a concept. Children grow up in "broken" homes when families who are unhealthy remain unhealthy, and fail to demonstrate for those children that sometimes doing the right thing means doing the hard thing. Children deserve to see their parents healthy and happy, and sometimes that may lie on the other side of a very tough decision. Nobody marries with the intention to divorce, but divorce is not a "failure". It's a decision. In life, we sometimes are faced with tough decisions; decisions that don't feel good; decisions that result in some very challenging circumstances.

That said, oftentimes the right decisions are the ones that come with such consequences. As a matter of fact, most circumstances will put us in the predicament where the right thing to do is the hard thing to do. Your therapist won't tell you to divorce your spouse, yet they may often try to encourage you to see these truths in the matter. Marriages don't fail, nor do they succeed. You are not a failure if you determine your marriage is detrimental to your health and separation is the next right thing.

The bottom line is that divorce is not a sign of failure any more than marriage is a sign of success.

Divorce isn't about blame; it's about acknowledging the sheer emotional chaos that accompanies the end of a significant relationship. It's a grieving process, a letting go of not just a person, but a shared history, dreams, and a future you once envisioned together. Think of it as mourning the death of a dream, a future, a partnership, the loss of an identity you once held as a 'couple.' It's a multifaceted grief, far more complex than simply missing someone.

One of the most common feelings is anger. Raging, all-consuming anger. Anger at your ex, anger at yourself, anger at the circumstances that led to this point. You might replay arguments in your head, dissecting every word, searching for that elusive "smoking gun" that proves you were right all along. But honestly, dwelling on who was "right" or "wrong" is rarely productive. It's a waste of valuable emotional energy that could be used for healing and moving forward. Think of it like this: you're caught in a traffic jam; screaming and honking won't get you there any faster.

Sadness, regardless of the circumstances, can almost always be expected. A deep, often overwhelming sadness that can creep in at any moment. It can manifest in unexpected ways—a song on the radio, a shared memory, even the smell of their favorite coffee can send you spiraling into a pit of melancholic reflection. It's okay to cry, to allow yourself to feel the sadness. Suppressing your emotions is like trying to hold a beach ball underwater; eventually, it's going to pop back up, and with greater force. Allow yourself the space to grieve, to process the loss, even if it feels like a slow, agonizing process. Remember, grief doesn't follow a neat, linear path; it's messy, unpredictable, and often exhausting. Don't expect it to be any different.

Some will experience confusion: a sheer disorientation of navigating a new reality. You might find yourself questioning everything –your decisions, your self-worth, your future. It's like suddenly finding yourself on a deserted island, with no map, no supplies, and no clear idea of how to get back to civilization. This is where self-compassion becomes crucial. Treat yourself with the same kindness and understanding you'd offer a friend going through a similar experience. Remind yourself that you're not alone, that this is a challenging but surmountable phase, and that you have the strength to navigate it.

Beyond the emotional rollercoaster, divorce often brings a wave of financial anxieties. Suddenly, you might be facing the prospect of splitting assets, managing debt, and creating a new budget from scratch. This can be incredibly stressful, especially if you were primarily dependent on your spouse's income or were less involved in managing the finances. Don't be afraid to seek professional help –a financial advisor can guide you through the complexities of dividing assets, creating a realistic budget, and planning for your future financial security.

Remember that navigating this phase is a marathon, not a sprint.

There will be good days and bad days, moments of clarity and moments of utter confusion. It's a process of healing, rebuilding, and rediscovering yourself. Self-care becomes paramount during this time. Prioritize your physical and mental health. Engage in activities that bring you joy, whether it's spending time in nature, practicing yoga, reading, listening to music, or simply taking a long, relaxing bath. Reconnect with friends and family, lean on your support system, and don't be afraid to seek professional help if you're struggling to cope. Therapy can provide a safe and supportive space to process your emotions, develop coping mechanisms, and navigate the challenges ahead.

Consider journaling as a tool for self-discovery. Writing down your thoughts and feelings can be a cathartic experience, helping you to process your emotions and gain a clearer understanding of your situation. Don't be afraid to be brutally honest with yourself; this is your space to express whatever you are feeling, without judgment.

You might discover patterns or insights that you weren't aware of before.

Examine the practical aspects as well. Develop a new routine, incorporating healthy habits into your daily life. This might include regular exercise, a balanced diet, and adequate sleep. These seemingly simple changes can have a profound impact on your physical and mental well-being, helping you to regain a sense of control and stability in your life.

Building a support network is essential. Reach out to trusted friends and family members, let them know you're going through a tough time, and ask for their support. Don't be afraid to ask for help; it's a sign of strength, not weakness. Surround yourself with people who uplift and encourage you, who celebrate your strengths and help you navigate your challenges.

Often, the financial aspects of divorce are a major source of stress. The uncertainty of the future can be overwhelming, especially if you are unsure about your financial resources or if the divorce proceedings are complicated. This is where seeking professional help becomes critical. Consult a financial advisor to help you understand your financial situation and develop a plan for your future financial security. They can assist you in managing debt, creating a realistic budget, and planning for long-term financial stability. Remember, there are resources available to help you navigate this aspect of divorce; it's not something you have to face alone.

The journey through divorce is rarely easy. There will be moments of doubt, moments of anger, moments of sheer exhaustion. But remember, you are not alone. Many people have gone through this experience and emerged stronger and more resilient on the other side. Embrace the process, allow yourself to grieve, and focus on rebuilding your life. With self-compassion, support, and the right resources, you can navigate this challenging phase and emerge a stronger, more empowered version of yourself. The future may seem uncertain, but it also holds the potential for new beginnings, for growth, and for a life that is even more fulfilling than the one you left behind. Remember, this is about creating a life you love, on your own terms. The chapter may be closing, but the story isn't over; it's just beginning a new and exciting chapter.

CoParenting and Shared Custody

So, you've navigated the emotional wreckage of divorce, acknowledged the grief, and started to pick up the pieces. But what if there are little pieces – tiny humans – caught in the wreckage?

That's where co-parenting comes in, a whole new level of complexity added to an already challenging situation. Let's be honest, the idea of maintaining a civil, even cordial, relationship with your ex-spouse after a bitter divorce often feels about as likely as finding a unicorn riding a bicycle in your backyard. Yet, it's often absolutely crucial for the well-being of your children.

Co-parenting isn't about being best friends; it's about establishing a functional partnership focused on the needs of your children. It's about setting aside personal feelings and grudges to create a stable and supportive environment for them. Think of it less like a blissful partnership and more like a well-oiled, if slightly rusty, machine. The goal isn't harmony, it's functionality. It's about getting the job done, even if it requires some grease and a few adjustments along the way.

One of the first hurdles is communication. After years of possibly strained or broken communication patterns, re-establishing healthy communication with your ex is a significant undertaking. The temptation to snipe through email, to engage in passive-aggressive Facebook posts, or to rely on the kids to relay messages is strong.

But resist this urge. This is where clear, concise, and direct communication becomes your lifeline. Consider scheduling regular calls or meetings, ideally without the children present. Focus on logistics – pick-up and drop-off times, school events, doctor's appointments, and extracurricular activities. Avoid getting sidetracked into old arguments or emotional outbursts. Think of it like a business meeting; stick to the agenda and try to treat it as a purely transactional event.

This requires a level of emotional maturity that can feel impossible to achieve when you're still reeling from the divorce. It's okay to feel angry, frustrated, or even resentful. But acknowledge those feelings without letting them dictate your interactions with your ex.
Consider writing down your feelings beforehand to help you stay composed during the conversations. Think of it as a

pre-game strategy to manage your reactions and emotions.

In many cases, the complexities of a divorce go far beyond simple disagreements. In my practice, I've worked with couples grappling with vastly different parenting styles, conflicting religious beliefs, and even allegations of abuse. These situations call for a much more structured approach, often involving mediation or legal intervention. Remember, your children's well-being is paramount, and if you cannot establish a functional co-parenting relationship on your own, seeking professional help is not a sign of weakness but a demonstration of your commitment to the well-being of your kids.

One client, whom we'll call "Sarah," found herself struggling to co-parent with her ex-husband after a particularly contentious divorce.

They had radically different approaches to discipline; he was a disciplinarian, while she preferred a more nurturing style. This created a constant battleground, confusing their children and leading to emotional distress. Through therapy, Sarah learned to separate her feelings about her ex from the needs of their children.

She and her ex-husband learned to collaborate, focusing on establishing clear, consistent boundaries, rather than arguing over the "best" approach. It wasn't easy, but through patient negotiation and compromise, they eventually managed to create a more unified, if somewhat different, approach to parenting.

The legal aspects of custody agreements can also be incredibly challenging. Different arrangements exist to meet varied family dynamics and needs. Sole custody grants one parent primary physical and legal custody, while the other parent has visitation rights. Joint legal custody implies that both parents share decision-making authority regarding the children's upbringing, even if one parent has primary physical custody. Joint physical custody means that children spend a roughly equal amount of time with each parent. Understanding the implications of each agreement is essential; you'll need to figure out what works best for your particular situation and your children's needs.

However, even with a solid agreement in place, disputes can still arise. A well-drafted parenting plan includes a clear division of responsibilities, a detailed schedule of visitation, and a conflict resolution mechanism. Think of it as a detailed blueprint for the co-parenting partnership. The plan should be reviewed and updated regularly, as the children grow, and their needs evolve. Remember, it's not a static document; it's a dynamic tool designed to adapt to your family's changing circumstances.

Creating clear boundaries is equally important. This goes beyond just logistical arrangements. It also involves defining how you will communicate with each other, how you'll deal with disagreements, and how you'll handle conflicting plans or unforeseen events. Establishing clear boundaries helps maintain a level of professionalism in your interactions, preventing things from becoming overly personal.

One common issue that emerges in co-parenting situations is the tendency of one parent to undermine the other. This can manifest in various ways, from subtle digs about the other parent's parenting style to outright attempts to turn the children against them. This is where mature behavior and a strong focus on the children's best interests are critical. Think of it as having the patience of a saint and the strategic skills of a master negotiator, all while feeling like you're being pulled apart in opposite directions.

Another scenario I've often witnessed is parents using children as messengers. Avoid this at all costs. Children should never be put in the middle of parental disputes. Keep your conversations about logistics and parenting separate from your personal feelings. Remember, the ultimate goal is to provide stability and consistency for your kids.

Finally, remember that seeking professional help is a sign of strength, not weakness. Family therapists can mediate disagreements, help parents establish clear communication strategies, and support both parents in navigating the complex emotional landscape of co-parenting. Remember, you're not alone in this, and seeking help will not only benefit you and your ex but, most importantly, your children. Co-parenting is a marathon, not a sprint; it demands patience, perseverance, and a commitment to putting your children's needs first. And yes, even a healthy dose of humor can help you navigate the inevitable bumps in the road.

Because let's face it, even the most well-oiled machines need occasional maintenance and a little bit of WD-40 to keep things running smoothly. The rewards, however, far outweigh the challenges. The ability to successfully co-parent provides stability and security for your children, enabling them to thrive despite the difficult changes in their family structure. It's about demonstrating to them that even in the midst of conflict, adults can find a way to cooperate for the sake of their well-being. And that's a lesson worth teaching, no matter what.

Rebuilding Your Life After Divorce

So, you've navigated the treacherous waters of divorce, perhaps even successfully charted the rocky terrain of co-parenting. Congratulations! You've survived a major life upheaval. But now what? The dust has settled, the legal battles (hopefully) are over, and you're staring at the wreckage—and your reflection in the shattered pieces. This is where the real work begins: rebuilding your life. And trust me, it's a project that deserves a detailed blueprint, not just a quick sketch.

The first thing to remember is that rebuilding isn't about instantly becoming a new, improved version of yourself. It's about consciously choosing to build something better, brick by brick, even if some of those bricks are a little rough around the edges. It's a marathon, not a sprint, and there will be days when you just want to curl up on the couch and binge-watch reality TV. And that's perfectly okay. Allow yourself those moments of self-compassion. You deserve them.

One of the most crucial aspects of rebuilding is self-care. This isn't about indulging in frivolous luxuries; it's about prioritizing your physical and emotional well-being. Think of it as preventative maintenance for your mental health. This might involve regular exercise—even a brisk walk can work wonders—a healthy diet, sufficient sleep, and mindfulness practices like meditation or yoga.

Find activities that nourish your soul, whether it's painting, gardening, reading, or spending time in nature. Remember those hobbies you neglected during the marriage? Dust them off and give them a try. You might discover a hidden talent or just rediscover a long-lost passion.

Developing new routines is another vital step. Divorce often throws our lives into disarray, leaving us with a gaping void where stability once existed. Creating new routines helps establish a sense of normalcy and predictability, even amidst the chaos. This could involve setting a regular wake-up time, planning healthy meals, or scheduling dedicated time for work, exercise, and relaxation.

Consistency is key here; even small, consistent steps can make a significant difference. Don't try to overhaul your entire life overnight. Start small and gradually build upon your successes.

Think of it as building a sturdy foundation for your new life.

Building a strong support system is also incredibly important. Lean on your friends and family; let them know you need their support. Don't be afraid to ask for help, whether it's for practical assistance or simply a listening ear. If you find yourself struggling to cope, consider seeking professional help. A therapist can provide a safe and non-judgmental space to process your emotions and develop coping mechanisms. Remember, seeking professional help is a sign of strength, not weakness. You wouldn't hesitate to seek medical help for a physical ailment; your mental health deserves the same level of care and attention.

Processing grief is a vital, albeit painful, part of the rebuilding process. Divorce is a significant loss, and it's essential to allow yourself to grieve the loss of the relationship, the life you had envisioned, and the future you once anticipated. This doesn't mean wallowing in sorrow indefinitely; it means acknowledging and accepting your feelings without judgment. Allow yourself to cry, to scream, to rage—whatever emotions surface, let them flow.

Journaling can be a powerful tool for processing your grief; it allows you to express your emotions without fear of judgment.

Talking to a trusted friend, family member, or therapist can also provide support and validation. Remember, healing takes time, and there's no set timeline for processing your grief. Be patient with yourself; allow yourself the time and space you need to heal.

Cultivating a positive self-image is crucial in rebuilding your life.

Divorce often leaves us feeling insecure, inadequate, and even worthless. It's essential to challenge these negative thoughts and beliefs. Focus on your strengths and accomplishments; remember all the things you're good at, and celebrate your successes, no matter how small they might seem. Practice self-compassion; treat yourself with the same kindness and understanding you would offer a friend going through a similar experience. Engage in activities that boost your self-esteem, such as setting and achieving personal goals, learning new skills, or volunteering in your community. Remember that you are worthy of love, happiness, and fulfillment, regardless of your relationship status.

Let's look at some real-life examples. I've worked with numerous clients who have successfully navigated the complexities of divorce and rebuilt fulfilling lives. One client, let's call her "Maria," found herself completely lost after her husband left her for another woman. She felt like a failure, a complete mess. Through therapy, Maria learned to process her grief, cultivate a positive self-image, and build a support system. She rediscovered her passion for painting, started taking classes, and eventually began selling her artwork. Today, Maria is a successful artist, happily remarried, and thriving.

Another client, "David," was devastated when his wife initiated divorce proceedings. He felt overwhelmed by the emotional and logistical challenges. David started by establishing new routines, focusing on exercise and healthy eating habits. He also joined a support group for men going through divorce, where he found a sense of camaraderie and understanding. David gradually rebuilt his life, focusing on his career, his relationships with his children, and his own personal growth. He's now living a fulfilling life, proving that it's possible to heal and thrive after a painful divorce.

Rebuilding your life after divorce is a journey, not a destination. It requires patience, perseverance, and a willingness to embrace the unknown. It's about taking small steps, celebrating your successes, and learning from your setbacks. It's about rediscovering yourself, your strengths, and your passions. It's about creating a life that is authentically yours, a life filled with joy, purpose, and fulfillment.

Remember, you are not alone in this journey; there is support available to you every step of the way. Embrace the challenges, celebrate the victories, and never underestimate your own resilience. The person you become after the divorce, stronger, wiser, more self-aware – that's a person worth celebrating. And yes, maybe even rewarding with a really good glass of wine. You've earned it.

Financial Planning Post-Divorce

Now that we've addressed the emotional and practical aspects of rebuilding your life post-divorce, let's tackle a crucial, often overlooked, element: your finances. Divorce is rarely a financially painless experience. In fact, it often throws your financial life into complete disarray, leaving you feeling overwhelmed, insecure, and perhaps even panicked. But don't despair! Just like rebuilding your emotional well-being, rebuilding your financial life is a process, a journey that requires planning, patience, and a healthy dose of realistic expectations.

The first step is often the most daunting: dividing your assets. This process can be complex, especially if your marriage involved significant assets like a house, investments, or a business. Unless you and your ex-spouse are remarkably amicable (and let's be honest, that's rarely the case post-divorce), you'll likely need the assistance of legal professionals. Attorneys specializing in family law can help navigate the legal complexities, ensuring a fair and equitable division of assets, according to your state's laws and your divorce agreement. Don't underestimate the value of legal counsel here; it's an investment in your future financial security. Think of it as purchasing a safety net, a way to protect yourself from potentially devastating financial consequences.

Beyond the legal aspects, obtaining a clear picture of your shared finances is paramount. This includes gathering all relevant financial documents: bank statements, tax returns, investment statements, loan agreements, credit card statements—the whole shebang. It's a tedious task, I know, but incredibly important. This comprehensive inventory will provide the foundation for your financial negotiations and future planning. You might find it helpful to organize these documents into easily accessible folders, both physical and digital, for easy access and reference.

Once you have a complete picture of your shared assets, you'll need to tackle the issue of debt. Joint credit cards, mortgages, loans—these all need to be addressed. The division of debt is usually determined during the divorce proceedings, based on the terms of your agreement or court orders. It's essential to understand your responsibility for each debt, to ensure you don't end up burdened with more than your fair share. Again, your legal counsel will be invaluable in navigating these complexities, protecting you from potentially crippling financial burdens. Remember, this isn't a time for impulsive decisions or guilt-driven generosity. Protect your future financial well-being.

Beyond the division of assets and debt, you'll need to create a new budget. This is where getting a realistic picture of your income and expenses is essential. Many people find themselves underestimating their expenses in the initial stages of post-divorce life, leading to financial strain down the line. Be honest with yourself; don't shy away from the uncomfortable truth of your financial situation. Use budgeting apps or spreadsheets to track your income and expenses meticulously. This will give you a clear understanding of where your money is going and will allow you to identify areas where you can cut back. And don't forget to factor in unexpected expenses. Life has a knack for throwing curveballs, so it's wise to build a financial buffer for those unexpected repairs, medical bills, or other life events.

Consider consulting a financial advisor. This isn't a luxury; it's a valuable investment in your financial future. A financial advisor can provide unbiased guidance, helping you create a realistic budget, develop a long-term financial plan, and manage your investments wisely. They can also help you understand your options regarding retirement planning, insurance, and estate planning. Think of a financial advisor as your financial coach, guiding you through the often-confusing world of finance. They can help you to navigate the complexities of post-divorce finances, ensuring you make informed decisions that will benefit you in the long run.

One of the most vital aspects of financial planning post-divorce is setting realistic financial goals. Don't set yourself up for failure by aiming for unattainable targets. Start small. Perhaps your initial goal is to build an emergency fund, three to six months' worth of living expenses. Once you've achieved that, you can set larger goals, such as paying down debt or investing in your retirement. Break down these larger goals into smaller, more manageable steps, celebrating each milestone along the way. This incremental approach prevents feelings of being overwhelmed, keeping you motivated and on track.

Remember the examples of Maria and David from earlier? Let's revisit their journeys, but this time through the lens of their financial rebuilding. Maria, after the emotional turmoil of her divorce, found herself struggling financially. She sought legal counsel to ensure a fair division of assets and then worked with a financial advisor to create a budget that allowed her to support herself and her children. She meticulously tracked her expenses, identified areas where she could save, and gradually rebuilt her financial stability. Her artistic passion not only provided emotional healing but also became a source of income, eventually leading to financial independence.

David, initially overwhelmed by the financial aspects of his divorce, took a different approach. He meticulously documented all financial accounts and debts, working closely with his attorney to ensure a clear understanding of his financial obligations. Then, he spent time educating himself on personal finance, seeking advice from friends and mentors. He learned about budgeting, investing, and debt management. While it was a slow process, this approach, combined with his renewed focus on his career, allowed him to regain control of his financial life. He proved that even with limited financial expertise, proactive steps can pave the way for a secure future.

Remember, financial recovery post-divorce is a marathon, not a sprint. There will be setbacks, unexpected expenses, and moments of frustration. But maintaining a positive mindset, seeking professional guidance when needed, and setting realistic goals are crucial. Your financial well-being is integral to your overall well-being, influencing your emotional state and your ability to move forward. Don't hesitate to seek help—from attorneys, financial advisors, and even trusted friends and family. Rebuilding your financial life is a testament to your strength, resilience, and commitment to a brighter future. And let's be honest, financial stability makes that celebratory glass of wine taste even sweeter.

You deserve it. You've earned it. And you're doing great. Keep going.

Dating and Relationships After Divorce
So, you've navigated the emotional rollercoaster and the financial minefield of divorce. Congratulations! You've emerged, perhaps slightly bruised but undeniably stronger. Now, the question on many minds—and hearts—is: dating. The prospect can feel daunting, even terrifying. After all, you've just been through a major life upheaval, a dismantling of a significant relationship. The thought of putting yourself back out there, vulnerable and open to potential rejection or heartbreak, can be enough to make anyone grab a pint of ice

cream and binge-watch old sitcom reruns. And that's perfectly okay! Allow yourself that time for self-care and healing. But eventually, for many, the desire for connection reemerges. So, let's explore this new terrain with a blend of realistic advice and a healthy dose of humor. Your therapist is not going to tell you not to move on.

The first step is often the hardest: self-reflection. Before you even think about swiping right or attending a mixer, take some time to understand yourself. What are your needs and wants in a relationship? What did you learn from your previous marriage? What are your non-negotiables? This isn't about dwelling on the past; it's about using it as a guide for the future. Imagine your past relationship as a GPS that took you on a scenic—and sometimes bumpy—route. You're now recalibrating your GPS for a new destination, a healthier, more fulfilling path.

A common pitfall is jumping back into the dating pool too soon. Healing takes time, and forcing yourself to date before you're ready can lead to unhealthy choices and a whole lot of emotional baggage being dumped into a new relationship—definitely not a recipe for success! Think of your heart as a delicate flower; you wouldn't force it to bloom before its time, would you? Give it the sun, water (self-care!), and time it needs to flourish.

When you do feel ready, start slow. Don't pressure yourself to find "the one" immediately. Consider dating as a process of exploration, a journey of discovery where you're learning about yourself and others. Think of it as a delicious tasting menu rather than a three-course meal; you get to sample different flavors and see what resonates with you. Online dating is a ubiquitous option in today's world. While it offers convenience and a wider pool of potential partners, it also has its challenges. Be mindful of red flags – inconsistencies in profiles, pressure to move things too fast, overly aggressive or controlling behavior. Trust your gut! If something feels off, it probably is. Remember, you're not just choosing a dating partner; you're choosing someone who could potentially be a significant part of your life.

Don't be afraid to be upfront and honest about your past. You don't need to share every detail of your divorce on the first date, but it's crucial to be transparent about your emotional and relationship history. This isn't about confessing your faults; it's about establishing authenticity and building trust. It's like taking off the heavy winter coat of your past – once you remove it, you feel so much more comfortable and open to new connections. Trying to hide or downplay your past is like trying to hide a giraffe in a closet– it's simply not going to work, and it will only create problems down the line.

Setting healthy boundaries is essential. This means understanding your limits and communicating them clearly. Don't feel pressured to do anything you're not comfortable with, whether it's physical intimacy, emotional vulnerability, or financial sharing. Boundaries aren't walls; they're fences that protect your garden— your heart, your time, and your well-being. Imagine them as well-placed guard dogs, politely but firmly protecting you from unwanted advances or unhealthy relationships.

Recognize red flags. These can manifest in many ways, from controlling behavior and jealousy to a lack of respect for your boundaries or past experiences. If you notice patterns of manipulation or disrespect, trust your intuition and don't make excuses for their behavior. This might seem like a tough lesson, but it's far better to recognize these early on and walk away than to invest time and emotion in a relationship that's ultimately going to cause you pain. Remember, you deserve respect, kindness, and a relationship built on mutual trust.

Building healthy relationships is about creating a space for open communication, trust, and mutual respect. It's about finding someone who supports your growth and shares your values. It's not about finding a perfect match; it's about finding someone who complements your imperfections. Healthy relationships are like good jazz – and improvisation of understanding, love, and compromise. Remember the good times, the laughter, the connection you're seeking. This helps maintain a positive and encouraging outlook.

Remember those budgeting apps and spreadsheets we talked about earlier? Well, they can be surprisingly useful in dating too. Not literally, of course, but in terms of investing your time and energy wisely. Don't overinvest in relationships that are clearly going nowhere. Know when to move on, when to cut your losses and preserve your emotional energy for something more promising.

Dating after divorce is a unique experience, often filled with both challenges and opportunities. It requires self-awareness, healthy boundaries, and a willingness to learn from the past. It's not a race; it's a journey. Allow yourself time to heal, reflect, and build a stronger, more resilient you. And remember, there's no shame in seeking support – whether it's from friends, family, a therapist, or a dating coach. The goal is not just to find a new partner, but to create a fulfilling life where you are happy, healthy, and whole. You deserve that. And when you find that, that first celebratory glass of wine will taste even sweeter.

You've earned it. Keep going. You're doing great.

Let's explore some real-world scenarios, keeping in mind that these are anonymized examples to illustrate common challenges and successful strategies:

Sarah's story: Sarah jumped back into dating almost immediately after her divorce, driven by a desire to prove to herself and her ex-husband that she was still desirable. She rushed into relationships, overlooking red flags, and constantly felt disappointment. It took a while, but Sarah learned to prioritize healing and self-reflection before seeking new connections.

Mark's story: Mark entered the dating world cautiously, prioritizing emotional well-being. He focused on building his confidence and setting clear boundaries, and he meticulously paid attention to red flags, saving himself heartbreak. He eventually found a partner who shared his values and respected his boundaries, resulting in a happy and fulfilling relationship.

Emily and David's story: Emily and David both found themselves hesitant to re-enter the dating scene. Emily sought therapy to navigate her emotional baggage, then joined a hiking group and slowly reconnected to socializing. David started with a dating app but emphasized communication and transparency from the start. Both found fulfilling connections by carefully choosing their methods and focusing on personal growth first.

These examples highlight the diverse paths to finding love after divorce. There is no "one-size-fits-all" approach. The key is self-awareness, patience, and a commitment to healthy relationship dynamics. Remember, the journey to finding love after divorce is about rediscovering yourself, prioritizing your well-being, and building a future based on trust and mutual respect. It's a journey worthy of celebration, and you've got this!

Your therapist won't tell you to divorce your spouse, but she will encourage you to consider your health and wellness a higher priority.

2. You Are Mentally Ill

Your therapist won't tell you that you have significant mental illness.

She will acknowledge and identify the symptoms and patterns of behaviors, but she won't tell you that you are mentally ill. She knows that a direct label can be jarring, and perhaps, in your case, unnecessary. Instead, she focuses on your experiences, your thoughts, and the emotions that arise. She wants to understand the 'why' behind your actions and the motivations that drive you. It is a delicate dance, this therapy, and she is careful with her steps.

Over time, she helps you navigate the maze of your mind, offering insights and tools to manage the chaos. You begin to see patterns emerge, connections between your thoughts and actions, and slowly, a sense of control returns. It is empowering, this knowledge, and you feel a weight lift as you realize that understanding is the first step to healing. The therapist's office becomes your sanctuary, a place where you can explore the depths of your mind without fear of judgment. She is a guide, helping you traverse the complex landscape of your thoughts, and together, you uncover the roots of your behaviors.

With each session, a new layer is peeled back, revealing a deeper understanding of yourself and your unique struggles. It is a journey of self-discovery, and you are committed to the path, knowing that each step brings you closer to a place of peace and acceptance. Outside the confines of the therapy room, you begin to apply the lessons learned. You notice the triggers, the warning signs, and you are equipped to handle them. Learning more about a diagnosis can de-stigmatize and decrease fears surrounding the label, allowing you the freedom to get beyond the initial shock and discover solutions sooner.

Depression isn't just feeling a bit blue after a bad day; it's a complex mental health condition that significantly impacts a person's thoughts, feelings, behaviors, and overall functioning. Think of it like this: sadness is a normal human emotion, like experiencing hunger. We all feel sad sometimes – after a loss, a disappointment, or even just a particularly gloomy Tuesday. Sadness is a fleeting emotion, a temporary dip in our emotional energy. Depression, on the other hand, is like persistent, gnawing hunger, a constant, pervasive feeling that doesn't simply dissipate with time. It's a deep and persistent emptiness that can feel utterly overwhelming.

Recognizing depression involves understanding its multifaceted nature. There's no single, universal symptom, making diagnosis a nuanced process that ideally involves a mental health professional. However, some common signs and symptoms can serve as red flags. Imagine a spectrum, with mild symptoms at one end and severe symptoms at the other. Someone experiencing mild depressive symptoms might feel persistently low in mood, lack motivation, or struggle with sleep disturbances. They might also experience a noticeable decrease in pleasure or interest in activities they once enjoyed – a condition known as anhedonia. Think of your favorite hobby, the one you once eagerly anticipated. Now imagine feeling utterly indifferent towards it, lacking the energy or enthusiasm to participate.

As we move towards the severe end of the spectrum, the symptoms intensify. Individuals might experience significant weight loss or gain, changes in appetite, feelings of worthlessness or excessive guilt, difficulty concentrating, recurrent thoughts of death or suicide, and significant impairment in social, occupational, or other important areas of functioning. Imagine trying to perform even the simplest tasks – like getting out of bed or showering – feeling like climbing Mount Everest. The weight of exhaustion, apathy, and despair can feel paralyzing. It's important to emphasize the diversity of depression's presentation. What might manifest as persistent sadness in one person might present as irritability or anger in another. Some individuals might experience periods of intense emotional pain, while others might describe a more numb or apathetic state. This variability underscores the importance of individualized assessment by a mental health professional. They can help differentiate between fleeting sadness and a clinical diagnosis of depression, taking into account the duration, severity, and impact of symptoms on daily life.

Consider this: John, a successful lawyer, found himself struggling to maintain his usual high-performance standards. He started missing deadlines, his once-sharp mind felt foggy, and he withdrew from social interactions. Initially, he attributed it to stress from a demanding workload. However, after several months of persistent low mood, fatigue, and an inability to find joy in activities he previously loved—like playing golf with his friends—he realized something more profound was happening. John's experience is a testament to the fact that depression can impact anyone, regardless of their professional achievements or social standing.

Conversely, Mary, a stay-at-home mom, began experiencing intense feelings of guilt and inadequacy. She felt overwhelmed by the demands of childcare, constantly comparing herself to other mothers on social media. Her once-vibrant personality became subdued, marked by tearfulness, irritability, and an inability to find pleasure in spending time with her children, a situation that fueled her guilt even further. Mary's experience highlights how societal pressures and personal expectations can contribute to the development of depression.

The impact of depression extends beyond the individual, significantly affecting families and loved ones. Imagine the ripple effect of depression within a family: a spouse struggling to cope with their partner's emotional distress, children witnessing the emotional turmoil of a parent, and the overall disruption to family dynamics. Supporting a loved one with depression requires patience, understanding, and often, a willingness to seek professional help for the entire family. It's crucial to remember that providing support for someone with depression does not mean fixing them. It means offering empathy, understanding, and encouragement to seek professional help.

Differentiating between situational sadness and clinical depression requires careful observation and consideration. Situational sadness typically stems from a specific event or circumstance, such as a job loss, the death of a loved one, or a relationship breakup. While these events undoubtedly cause significant emotional distress, the sadness associated with them is generally time-limited and resolves with appropriate coping mechanisms and emotional support. It's like a storm that passes, leaving behind clouds, but eventually, the sun shines again.

In contrast, clinical depression is a persistent and pervasive state of low mood that significantly interferes with daily functioning. The triggers may or may not be readily identifiable, and the intensity and duration of the symptoms distinguish it from situational sadness. This is a prolonged, unrelenting grey cloud, constantly casting a shadow over every aspect of life.

Many individuals with depression grapple with the stigma associated with mental illness. This stigma can prevent them from seeking help, leading to a worsening of their condition. It's a vicious cycle, fueled by societal misconceptions and fear of judgment. It's important to remember that seeking help is a sign of strength, not weakness. It demonstrates a proactive commitment to one's well-being.

Early intervention is crucial in managing depression effectively. The earlier a diagnosis is made and treatment is initiated, the better the prognosis. Treatment approaches can vary, but common options include therapy, medication, or a combination of both. Therapy, particularly cognitive behavioral therapy (CBT), helps individuals identify and challenge negative thought patterns and develop healthier coping mechanisms. Medication can help regulate brain chemistry and alleviate some of the symptoms.

It's vital to emphasize that the recovery process from depression is not linear. It's often a journey filled with ups and downs, setbacks and progress. There will be days when the symptoms feel overwhelming, and there will be days when a glimmer of hope emerges. Patience, self-compassion, and consistent engagement with the treatment plan are vital for achieving long-term recovery.

Let's revisit Sarah's story from chapter one. The challenges she faced in dating were compounded by an underlying depression she hadn't acknowledged. Her impulsivity, inability to set boundaries, and desperate need for validation stemmed from a deeper emotional struggle. Once she addressed her depression through therapy and medication, she was better equipped to navigate the complexities of dating and build healthier relationships.

Seeking help can feel daunting but understanding that you're not alone in your struggle is a critical first step. Many resources are available, from mental health professionals to support groups and online communities. Reaching out to a friend, family member, or therapist can create a pathway to recovery. Take that initial step; it could be the start of your journey to a happier, healthier you. You deserve it, and you are worth it.

Anxiety Disorder: Types and Treatments

Now that we've explored the complexities of depression, let's turn our attention to another common mental health challenge: anxiety. While seemingly different from depression, anxiety and depression often coexist, creating a complex interplay of emotional and psychological difficulties. Think of them as two dancers in a sometimes chaotic tango, each influencing and impacting the other. Understanding the nuances of anxiety is crucial for effective management and improved overall well-being.

Anxiety, unlike the occasional pre-presentation jitters or the butterflies before a first date, is characterized by persistent and excessive worry, fear, and apprehension. It's that nagging feeling of unease that refuses to let go, casting a shadow over even the most mundane aspects of life. Imagine this feeling clinging to you like a persistent shadow, influencing your thoughts, behaviors and decisions. This persistent state of heightened arousal can significantly disrupt daily life, impacting relationships, work performance, and overall quality of life.

It's important to distinguish between normal anxiety—a natural human response to stressful situations—and an anxiety disorder. Healthy anxiety is a fleeting emotion, a temporary response to a perceived threat. It helps us navigate challenging situations, motivating us to study for an exam or prepare for a job interview. It's the fuel that pushes us to perform at our best, acting as a helpful catalyst under pressure.

Anxiety disorders, however, represent a more significant problem, a relentless and pervasive state of worry that surpasses healthy levels of apprehension. The intensity and duration of the anxiety, combined with the impact on daily functioning, are key differentiators. Anxiety disorders encompass a spectrum of conditions, each with its own unique characteristics and symptoms. Let's explore some of the most common types:

Generalized Anxiety Disorder (GAD): Picture this: you're constantly worrying, fretting about practically everything. Work, family, finances, health – even seemingly inconsequential matters –become sources of relentless anxiety.

The worry is excessive, persistent, and difficult to control. It's a constant mental chatter, a background hum of unease that permeates your everyday existence. Individuals with GAD often experience physical symptoms as well, such as muscle tension, fatigue, sleep disturbances, and irritability. Imagine the feeling of being perpetually on edge, your body tense, your mind racing.

Panic Disorder: This involves unexpected and recurrent panic attacks. A panic attack is a sudden surge of intense fear that escalates rapidly, creating a feeling of impending doom or catastrophe. Physical symptoms such as rapid heartbeat, shortness of breath, chest pain, dizziness, and sweating are common. Imagine experiencing a sudden surge of terror without any apparent reason, feeling overwhelmed and completely out of control. The fear of having another attack can lead to significant avoidance behaviors, impacting daily routines and social interactions.

Specific Phobias: These are persistent and excessive fears of specific objects, situations, or activities. This could include anything from fear of spiders (arachnophobia) or heights (acrophobia) to fear of enclosed spaces (claustrophobia) or flying (aviophobia). These phobias cause significant distress and disrupt daily routines, often leading to avoidance behaviors. Imagine the irrational, paralyzing terror triggered by the mere sight or thought of your specific phobia. It's not just mild discomfort; it's a debilitating fear that dictates your choices and behaviors.

Obsessive-Compulsive Disorder (OCD): This is characterized by intrusive, unwanted thoughts (obsessions) and repetitive behaviors or mental acts (compulsions) that are performed to reduce anxiety associated with those obsessions. Obsessions can involve contamination fears, intrusive aggressive or sexual thoughts, or concerns about symmetry and order. Compulsions are repetitive behaviors like excessive hand washing, checking, counting, or arranging objects. Imagine the constant struggle against intrusive thoughts, the repetitive actions driven by the desperate need to alleviate anxiety. It's a relentless internal battle that can be both exhausting and debilitating.

Post-Traumatic Stress Disorder (PTSD):
This develops following exposure to a traumatic event such as a serious accident, assault, natural disaster, or combat experience. PTSD is characterized by intrusive memories of the traumatic event, nightmares, flashbacks, avoidance behaviors, and significant emotional distress. Imagine the persistent haunting of a traumatic memory, the reliving of the horror in vivid detail, the constant state of hypervigilance and fear. It is a condition that profoundly impacts a person's ability to cope with daily life. The most important thing to remember about PTSD is that it is not determined by the event that was experienced, but instead *how the nervous system responds to it*. The treatments for anxiety disorders are multifaceted and tailored to the individual's specific needs

and the type of anxiety they are experiencing. Many approaches are effective and often used in combination.

Therapy: Cognitive Behavioral Therapy (CBT) is a highly effective treatment for anxiety disorders. CBT helps individuals identify and challenge negative thought patterns and develop healthier coping mechanisms. It's like restructuring the mental framework that fuels the anxiety response. Exposure therapy, a component of CBT, involves gradually exposing individuals to their feared stimuli or situations in a safe and controlled environment. It's a systematic desensitization, helping individuals confront their fears and reduce avoidance behaviors.

Medication: Anti-anxiety medications, such as benzodiazepines, can provide short-term relief from anxiety symptoms, but they're typically not recommended for long-term use due to the risk of dependence and side effects. Antidepressants, such as selective serotonin reuptake inhibitors (SSRIs) and serotonin-norepinephrine reuptake inhibitors

(SNRIs), are often effective in treating anxiety disorders, particularly when used in conjunction with therapy.

These medications help regulate brain chemistry, reducing the intensity and frequency of anxiety symptoms.

Relaxation Techniques: Practicing relaxation techniques such as deep breathing exercises, meditation, progressive muscle relaxation, and yoga can help manage anxiety symptoms. These techniques help regulate the body's physiological response to stress, reducing the intensity of physical symptoms associated with anxiety. Imagine learning to control your breath, to calm your racing heart, to find moments of stillness amidst the storm of anxiety.

Lifestyle Changes: Adopting healthy lifestyle changes such as regular exercise, a balanced diet, sufficient sleep, and limiting caffeine and alcohol intake can significantly impact anxiety levels. These changes help regulate the body's overall functioning, making it more resilient to stress. Imagine the profound impact of a healthy lifestyle on

reducing the vulnerability to anxiety
triggers.

Support Groups: Connecting with others
who share similar experiences can provide
invaluable support and encouragement.
Sharing your experiences, receiving
empathy, and learning coping strategies
from others in a supportive environment can
enhance your ability to manage your
anxiety.
Remember, recognizing the signs of anxiety
and seeking professional help is a sign of
strength, not weakness. The sooner you
address your anxiety, the sooner you can
begin your journey toward managing your
symptoms and reclaiming your life. Early
intervention is crucial for preventing anxiety
from becoming debilitating and impacting
all aspects of your life.

Let's revisit the analogy of the
mental health landscape. We've navigated
the challenging terrain of depression, and
now we're exploring the treacherous slopes
of anxiety. Both conditions can be difficult
to climb, but with the right tools—therapy,

medication, lifestyle changes, and a strong support system—you can reach the summit, enjoying a panoramic view of a healthier, happier you. Don't let anxiety control you; take control of your anxiety. You have the power within you to navigate this challenging terrain and create a life filled with less worry and more joy. Your well-being matters, and seeking help is a testament to your strength and commitment to a better future.

Bipolar Disorder: The High Highs, The Low Lows

Now that we've journeyed through the landscapes of depression and anxiety, let's tackle another significant mental health challenge: bipolar disorder. If depression and anxiety are like individual storms, bipolar disorder is more like a volatile, unpredictable weather system—a whirlwind of extreme mood swings that can leave individuals and their loved ones feeling utterly bewildered. It's a condition that throws curveballs, often without warning, making consistency and predictability feel like a distant dream.

Bipolar disorder, once known as manic-depressive illness, is a chronic condition characterized by extreme shifts in mood, energy, and activity levels. These shifts can range from periods of intense elation and hyperactivity (mania or hypomania) to periods of profound sadness and despair (depression). Imagine a rollercoaster that never stops, with exhilarating highs plummeting into terrifying lows. That's the experience for many living with bipolar disorder.

The experience of mania can be thrilling, at least initially. Individuals might feel incredibly energized, creative, and productive. Their minds race with ideas, they're bursting with energy, and sleep often seems unnecessary. It's a time of heightened confidence, sometimes bordering on grandiosity. They might take on ambitious projects, spend money recklessly, engage in risky behaviors, or experience a decreased need for sleep. However, this exhilarating high comes at a cost. This heightened state can be exhausting, ultimately leading to burnout and a subsequent crash into depression. The manic phase can also disrupt relationships and lead to impulsive decisions with lasting negative consequences.

Think of it as a powerful engine running full throttle, eventually sputtering and breaking down. The depressive episodes, on the other hand, are the stark opposite. These periods are marked by profound sadness, loss of interest in activities once enjoyed, fatigue, sleep disturbances, changes in appetite, and difficulty concentrating. The joy and energy of the manic phase seem like a distant memory, replaced by feelings of hopelessness and worthlessness. It's a debilitating state that can significantly impact daily functioning, leading to withdrawal from social interactions, decreased productivity, and potential thoughts of self-harm or suicide. It's a dark cloud that hangs heavy, suffocating the light and joy from life.

The intensity and duration of these mood swings vary greatly from person to person. Some individuals experience rapid cycling, with multiple mood shifts within a short period, while others may have longer periods of stability interspersed with more extreme episodes.

There's no typical bipolar experience; each person's journey is unique. This lack of predictability is a significant challenge for both the individual and their support system. The diagnosis of bipolar disorder is complex and requires a thorough evaluation by a mental health professional. There's no single test to diagnose it; instead, clinicians rely on a combination of symptom assessment, medical history, and observation to arrive at a diagnosis. It's essential to rule out other conditions that might present with similar symptoms. The diagnostic process can be challenging, with many individuals experiencing years of misdiagnosis or delays before receiving appropriate care.

Effective management of bipolar disorder typically involves a combination of medication, therapy, and lifestyle adjustments. Medication is often crucial for stabilizing mood swings and preventing future episodes. Mood stabilizers, antipsychotics, and antidepressants are commonly prescribed, depending on the individual's specific needs and the type of episode they're experiencing. It's important to understand that finding the right medication and dosage can take time, and it requires close collaboration with a psychiatrist. It's a bit like finding the right key to unlock a complex lock – it might take several tries.

Therapy, particularly cognitive behavioral therapy (CBT) and interpersonal and social rhythm therapy (IPSRT), plays a significant role in managing bipolar disorder. CBT helps individuals identify and challenge negative thought patterns and develop healthier coping mechanisms. IPSRT focuses on stabilizing daily routines, including sleep patterns, social interactions, and mealtimes, which can help reduce the severity and frequency of mood swings.

Imagine these therapies as tools to build a more stable and resilient foundation for navigating the unpredictable weather of bipolar disorder. Beyond medication and therapy, lifestyle adjustments are equally critical. This includes maintaining a regular sleep schedule, engaging in regular physical activity, eating a healthy diet, minimizing stress, and limiting the consumption of alcohol and caffeine. These lifestyle changes aren't quick fixes, but consistent efforts in these areas can contribute significantly to long-term stability. Think of them as the supportive pillars that reinforce the foundation built by medication and therapy.

Self-monitoring is also vital for individuals with bipolar disorder. Keeping a mood diary, tracking symptoms, and identifying triggers can help individuals and their healthcare providers gain insights into patterns and develop personalized strategies for managing episodes. This self-awareness is powerful in predicting and responding to shifts in mood.

Family and social support are crucial. Educating family and friends about bipolar disorder can significantly improve understanding and reduce stigma. Support groups offer valuable opportunities for individuals to connect with others who share similar experiences, providing a sense of community and shared understanding. This support system acts as a safety net, offering a sense of belonging and resilience during challenging times.

The journey with bipolar disorder is a marathon, not a sprint. It requires patience, persistence, and a strong support system. There will be ups and downs, challenges and triumphs. However, with the right treatment plan, self-management strategies, and unwavering support, individuals with bipolar disorder can lead fulfilling and meaningful lives. Many people successfully manage their symptoms and thrive, contributing to their communities and pursuing their passions.

Let's consider some examples, remembering that every individual's experience is unique: one person might find that maintaining a consistent exercise routine significantly reduces the severity of their depressive episodes. Another might discover that adhering to a strict sleep schedule is crucial for preventing manic episodes. Yet another might find that engaging in creative pursuits, like painting or writing, helps them express their emotions and navigate the emotional roller coaster.

The key takeaway here is that effective management of bipolar disorder is an ongoing process, a journey of self-discovery and adaptation. It's about finding the right combination of strategies that work best for the individual. It's not about eliminating mood swings entirely, but about learning to navigate them with grace and resilience. It's about accepting the challenges while celebrating the strengths. It's about building a life that acknowledges the complexities of the condition while embracing the richness of human experience. It's about understanding that seeking help is not a sign of weakness but a testament to strength and a commitment to a healthier, more balanced life. The journey may be challenging, but it is a journey worth embarking on. With the right tools and support, individuals with bipolar disorder can not only manage their condition but also live vibrant and fulfilling lives. The path to wellness is paved with self-awareness, professional guidance, and the unwavering support of loved ones. Remember, you're not alone in this journey. There are resources, support systems, and professionals dedicated to helping you navigate this complex landscape and create a life filled with purpose and joy.

The path to recovery is rarely linear. It's characterized by periods of improvement and setbacks, requiring ongoing vigilance and adaptation. But the journey is worth taking. With the right support system, commitment to treatment, and a proactive approach, individuals with schizophrenia can learn to manage their symptoms and build a life filled with purpose, connection, and hope.

Remember, you are not alone. There are resources, professionals, and support systems dedicated to helping you navigate this challenging journey and build a fulfilling and meaningful life.

Seeking Professional Help for Mental Illness

Now that we've explored the intricacies of some common mental illness conditions, let's shift our focus to the crucial next step: seeking professional help. This isn't about weakness; it's about strategic self-care. Think of it like this: you wouldn't try to fix a leaky roof with a band-aid, would you?

Similarly, navigating the complexities of mental illness requires specialized expertise. A qualified therapist or counselor is your skilled roofer, equipped to handle the problem effectively.

Finding the right therapist can feel like searching for a needle in a haystack, especially when you're already feeling overwhelmed. But it's a search absolutely worth undertaking. Don't be afraid to shop around – finding a good therapeutic fit is key to a successful journey. Think of it like trying on shoes – some might look great, but if they don't feel right, they're not going to be comfortable for the long haul.

One of the first hurdles is often insurance coverage. Navigating the world of insurance benefits and mental health coverage can feel like deciphering hieroglyphics. Don't be discouraged! Most insurance plans provide at least some coverage for mental health services. Start by contacting your insurance provider directly. Ask specific questions about your coverage: What is your annual out-of-pocket maximum for mental health services? How many sessions are covered per year? Is there a network of providers you must use? Knowing the answers to these questions will help you budget and plan effectively.

Many therapists offer a free 15-minute consultation, a sort of "meet and greet" to gauge compatibility. This is invaluable! Use this time to ask questions, assess their approach, and see if you feel comfortable opening up to them. It's okay to have a gut feeling – if something doesn't feel quite right, don't hesitate to move on. Trust your intuition. A good therapist-client relationship is built on trust, mutual respect, and open communication – the foundation upon which healing is built.

Consider your specific needs when selecting a therapist. Do you prefer someone with experience in a particular area, such as trauma, anxiety, or depression? Do you need someone who uses a specific therapeutic modality, like Cognitive Behavioral Therapy (CBT), Dialectical Behavior Therapy (DBT), or psychodynamic therapy? Researching different therapeutic approaches can help you make an informed decision and match your needs with a practitioner's expertise.

Remember, self-advocacy is paramount. Don't be afraid to express your needs and preferences to your therapist. If something isn't working, be honest and open about it. A good therapist will welcome your feedback and adjust their approach as needed. It's a collaborative partnership, not a one-way street. The therapeutic relationship is a dynamic process; it evolves and adapts as your needs change.

Beyond individual therapy, consider exploring other support systems. Support groups offer a safe and validating space to connect with others facing similar challenges. Sharing experiences and hearing from others can alleviate feelings of isolation and provide a sense of community. Finding others who understand can be immensely validating and empowering. There is strength in numbers, a shared sense of navigating the complexities of life. Family therapy can be incredibly helpful, especially if your mental health is impacting your relationships. It provides a forum for open communication, conflict resolution, and improving family dynamics. It helps families learn to support each other effectively. A strong support network at home can often be the linchpin for successful mental health management. Building a supportive therapeutic relationship is a journey, not a destination. It takes time, trust, and open communication.

Remember, you're not alone in this. Millions of people seek professional help for mental illness, and you are not an exception, but a testament to the growing acknowledgment and acceptance of mental health needs. Remember those self-care strategies we discussed earlier? They're not just add-ons; they are fundamental components of your overall well-being and are crucial for supporting the work you're doing with your therapist. Think of them as the supporting pillars that hold up the entire structure of your mental health.

Imagine your mental health as a house. The foundation is your self-care routines, the walls are your therapeutic sessions, and the roof is the support you receive from your loved ones and community. A solid foundation, consistently maintained, is what allows the house to withstand storms and continue standing strong.

The journey toward better mental health is a marathon, not a sprint.

Be patient with yourself and the process. Therapy isn't a quick fix; it's an ongoing investment in your well-being. There will be ups and downs, breakthroughs and setbacks, and that's perfectly normal. It's a testament to the multifaceted nature of the human experience.

Celebrate the small victories and learn from the challenges.

Finding professional help is a sign of strength, not weakness. It's about proactively addressing your needs and investing in your well-being. It's about recognizing that seeking professional support is a crucial element of self-care. And it's about understanding that you don't have to face these challenges alone. There are people who care and resources available to help you on your journey.

Remember, your mental health is as important as your physical health. Don't hesitate to reach out for support when you need it.

You deserve to live a life free from the constraints of untreated mental illness. Take that first step and discover the power of seeking help. The path may be challenging at times, but with the right support, the journey towards a healthier, happier you is well within reach. And remember, even the most experienced mountain climbers need experienced guides to reach the peak. Your therapist is your experienced guide. Now go get that mountain conquered.

Your therapist won't call you *mentally ill*, but she'll do all that she can to encourage you to get the treatment you deserve.

3. You're An Asshole

Your therapist won't tell you you're an asshole. But if you are, therapy can help.

Often the best way to learn about oneself is to verbalize your story to another person. Hearing yourself explain, out loud, the ins and outs of your day, your encounters, the choices you made and the people you bailed on can offer great personal insight into how one treats others in their world. Sometimes, you learn something and change. Other times, your therapist wants to shake you and say *"Be a better person!"*

Effective communication in intimate relationships isn't about flawlessly articulating every thought or perfectly resolving every conflict. It's about creating a safe space for vulnerability, honesty, and mutual understanding. It's about actively listening, not just waiting for your turn to speak. It's about expressing needs and desires clearly and respectfully, while simultaneously understanding and validating the needs and desires of your partner. It's a dance, a continuous process of give-and-take, of learning and adapting.

One of the biggest hurdles to effective communication is the tendency to jump to conclusions, to fill in the blanks with our own assumptions and interpretations rather than seeking clarification. This often leads to misunderstandings, hurt feelings, and resentment. For instance, imagine a scenario where one partner works late unexpectedly. The other partner might immediately assume the worst – that their partner is neglecting them, losing interest, or even having an affair. This assumption, fueled by insecurity and lack of communication, can escalate into a significant conflict. However, if the partner had simply asked, "Honey, what kept you so late?" the entire situation could have been avoided. The late arrival may have been due to a work emergency, a traffic accident, or something equally innocuous.

This highlights the importance of active listening – truly hearing what your partner is saying, both verbally and nonverbally. It means paying attention to their tone of voice, their body language, and their emotional state. It means asking clarifying questions to ensure you understand their perspective fully, rather than simply assuming you know what they mean.

Sometimes, this might involve repeating back what you've heard to confirm your understanding:

"So, what I'm hearing you say is..." This technique, known as paraphrasing, is a powerful tool for ensuring mutual understanding and preventing misinterpretations.

Another common communication roadblock is criticism. We often criticize our partners, focusing on their flaws and shortcomings rather than expressing our needs and feelings constructively.

Instead of saying, "You're always so messy!" try phrasing it as, "I feel overwhelmed when the house is cluttered, and I'd really appreciate it if we could work together to keep things tidy." Notice the shift from blaming ("You're always...") to expressing your own feelings ("I feel...") and outlining a clear, actionable request. This approach is far more likely to result in a positive outcome than a critical and accusatory statement.

Conflict is inevitable in any relationship, but how we navigate those conflicts determines the strength and resilience of the bond. It's essential to approach conflict as an opportunity for growth and understanding, rather than a battle to be won. This requires emotional regulation – the ability to manage your own emotions during tense moments. It also requires empathy, the ability to step into your partner's shoes and understand their perspective, even if you don't agree with it.

Healthy conflict resolution often involves compromise and negotiation. It's about finding solutions that work for both partners, rather than imposing your will on the other person. It is crucial to remember that compromise isn't about giving up on what's important to you, but rather finding creative solutions that meet both partners' needs. This might involve brainstorming together to find alternative solutions, or simply acknowledging each other's feelings and validating their perspectives, even when you don't agree.

Nonverbal communication plays a surprisingly significant role in intimate relationships. Body language, tone of voice, and facial expressions often speak louder than words. If your words say "I love you," but your tone is sarcastic and your body language is withdrawn, your message will be lost or even misinterpreted. Paying attention to your own nonverbal cues, as well as your partner's, is crucial for effective communication.

Maintaining open and honest communication requires ongoing effort and commitment. It's not something that happens overnight; it's a skill that needs to be practiced and refined over time. Regular check-ins, where you discuss your feelings, needs, and concerns, are invaluable for maintaining intimacy and preventing small issues from escalating into larger conflicts. This could involve scheduled "couple time" or simply taking a few minutes each day to connect and check in with each other.

One practical technique is to schedule regular "date nights." These aren't just about romantic dinners; they're about intentionally setting aside time to connect and engage with each other without distractions. This dedicated time allows for focused conversation, allowing for open communication and deep understanding. Furthermore, incorporating shared activities can strengthen the connection, creating shared memories and experiences that form the bedrock of a strong relationship. Furthermore, remember the importance of appreciating your partner. Expressing gratitude and acknowledging your partner's contributions, both big and small, fosters a positive and loving environment. A simple "thank you" or a heartfelt compliment can go a long way in strengthening your connection and building a supportive atmosphere. This simple act of appreciation can dramatically improve the emotional climate of the relationship.

Building strong communication skills takes conscious effort and practice. It may involve seeking professional help, like couples therapy, if you're struggling to navigate conflict or build a deeper connection. A therapist can provide a neutral space to work through challenges, offering guidance and tools to improve communication patterns and foster intimacy.

In conclusion, strong communication and connection are the cornerstones of a thriving intimate relationship. By actively practicing effective communication skills, navigating conflicts constructively, and prioritizing mutual understanding and appreciation, you can build a strong and resilient bond with your partner. This strengthens not only your relationship but also enhances your overall well-being and satisfaction with life, creating a harmonious balance between your financial goals and the emotional richness of your relationships. The investment in your relationship, much like investing wisely in your finances, will yield dividends far exceeding the initial effort.

Conflict Resolution in Relationships

Conflict is an inevitable part of any relationship, much like taxes or that inexplicable urge to buy another pair of shoes you'll probably never wear. The key isn't to avoid conflict entirely – that's about as realistic as achieving world peace by next Tuesday – but to learn how to navigate it effectively. Think of conflict as a relationship workout; it strengthens the emotional muscles if handled correctly.

If mishandled, well, you end up with a strained relationship and possibly a therapist's bill.

The first step towards healthy conflict resolution is recognizing that conflict isn't a sign of failure. It's actually a sign that you and your partner are engaging with each other, sharing your thoughts and feelings, and trying to work towards a common understanding. It's the avoidance of conflict that often breeds resentment and ultimately erodes the foundation of the relationship. It's like letting that leaky faucet drip for months instead of fixing it; eventually, you'll have a bigger problem on your hands.

Empathy is your superpower here. It's the ability to step into your partner's shoes, to see the world from their perspective, even if you fundamentally disagree with their viewpoint. Imagine you're arguing about the dishwasher loading technique (a classic!). Instead of launching into a tirade about the "correct" method, try understanding why your partner loads it the way they do. Maybe they're prioritizing speed, or perhaps they have a specific method that works for their organizational style. Understanding their reasoning, even if it frustrates you, allows for a more productive conversation.

Active listening is another crucial element. This isn't simply hearing your partner's words; it's truly understanding their message, both verbal and nonverbal. It involves paying attention to their tone of voice, their body language, and the emotions behind their words. This requires you to silence your internal monologue – that little voice constantly crafting your witty retort – and focus solely on understanding your partner. Think of it as giving your partner your full, undivided attention, like you would to a captivating Netflix show...

except, you know, the stakes are a little higher.

Paraphrasing is a fantastic tool for active listening. It involves summarizing your partner's point in your own words to ensure you've understood correctly. For example, if your partner says, "I feel frustrated when you don't help with the chores," you could respond with, "So, what I'm hearing is that you feel unsupported when it comes to household tasks, and that makes you feel frustrated." This shows your partner that you're paying attention, and it gives them an opportunity to clarify if you've missed anything. It's like a relationship quality check, ensuring you're both on the same page.

Constructive communication is about expressing your feelings and needs without resorting to blame or criticism. Instead of attacking your partner with accusations like, "You never listen to me!" try expressing your feelings using "I" statements. For example, "I feel unheard when I share my concerns," or "I feel frustrated when I'm constantly doing all the housework." This shifts the focus from blaming your partner to expressing your own experience. It transforms the conversation from a battlefield into a collaborative problem-solving session. It's the difference between yelling at the traffic jam and calmly finding an alternate route.

Compromise is the cornerstone of healthy conflict resolution. It's about finding a solution that works for both of you, even if it means making concessions. This isn't about surrendering your needs or principles, but about finding creative solutions that meet both your needs. Maybe it's taking turns with household chores, or perhaps it's agreeing to disagree on certain issues. Remember, a successful compromise is a win-win situation, not a competition to see who can concede the least. It's like negotiating a peace treaty, not a land grab.

Conflict resolution often necessitates identifying the underlying issues. A seemingly simple argument about who left the toilet seat up might be masking deeper issues like resentment, unequal workloads, or a lack of feeling appreciated. Digging beneath the surface to find the root cause of the conflict will often lead to a more lasting resolution. It's like a detective solving a mystery; you need to find the clues to uncover the real culprit.

Taking breaks is perfectly acceptable, especially during heated arguments. It's not giving up; it's acknowledging that emotional regulation is a crucial skill. When tempers flare, take a few minutes to cool off before resuming the conversation. This prevents the argument from escalating into a full-blown war, and allows you both to approach the issue with a clearer head. It's akin to hitting the pause button on a stressful movie – it allows you to regroup and approach it with a fresher perspective.

Seek professional help when needed. Couples therapy can provide a neutral space to work through conflict and develop better communication skills. A therapist can offer guidance, tools, and strategies for navigating challenging situations. Just like seeking help from a financial advisor for your investments, consulting a therapist is an investment in the health of your relationship. It's acknowledging that you value your relationship enough to seek expert guidance when facing difficulties.

Learn to forgive. Holding onto grudges will only poison your relationship and prevent you from moving forward. Forgiveness isn't about condoning hurtful behavior but about releasing the anger and resentment that prevents healing. It's about freeing yourself from the burden of negativity and creating space for growth and understanding. It's about choosing to let go of the past and focus on building a stronger future together.

Finally, remember that healthy conflict resolution is a skill that takes time and practice. There will be ups and downs, and there will be times when you stumble. The important thing is to learn from your mistakes, to keep practicing, and to remember that a strong relationship is built on mutual respect, understanding, and the willingness to navigate conflict constructively. It's a marathon, not a sprint. It's about patience, persistence, and a shared commitment to building a stronger, healthier, and more fulfilling partnership. Embrace the challenges, learn from the conflicts, and savor the journey. After all, a little friction can make the bond even stronger. Like a well-worn pair of jeans, the relationship's imperfections only add to its character.

Physical Intimacy and Emotional Intimacy

We've talked about navigating conflict, a crucial aspect of any relationship. Think of it as the relationship equivalent of clearing out your gutters – necessary for healthy flow. But beyond the occasional squabble over the remote or whose turn it is to walk the dog, there's another equally vital component: intimacy. And intimacy isn't just one thing; it's a dynamic duo, a well-oiled machine powered by both physical and emotional connection. Get one running smoothly, and the other often follows suit, but neglect either, and the whole system sputters.

Physical intimacy is often the first thing that springs to mind when we discuss this topic. It's the tangible connection, the warm embrace, the gentle touch, the passionate kiss. It's the language of the body, expressing love and affection in a way that words sometimes can't. This doesn't necessarily mean wild, passionate encounters every night (though those can be fantastic!). Physical intimacy encompasses a broad spectrum, from holding hands while watching a movie to cuddling on the couch to the more intimate physical expressions of love. The key is to foster a sense of comfort and ease within this shared physical space. It's about creating a safe haven where both partners feel accepted and appreciated, flaws and all.

Think of it like this: you wouldn't just jump into a freezing cold lake without easing your way in, would you? The same applies to physical intimacy. It's about gradually building a foundation of trust and comfort, a slow and steady climb towards deeper connection. Rushing into intense physical displays of affection before a strong emotional foundation is in place can lead to discomfort and potential disconnect. It's like attempting to build a house on quicksand – eventually, the whole structure is going to collapse.

But what if the spark fades? What if the routines of daily life overshadow the physical connection? This is entirely normal, and absolutely fixable. It's not a sign of a failing relationship; it's a call for recalibration. Schedule regular "date nights," even if it's just an hour of uninterrupted time together. Put away the phones, turn off the TV, and focus on each other. Try a new hobby together, learn to tango, or even just have a picnic in the park. Rediscovering shared interests can re-ignite the flame of physical intimacy. Remember the thrill of those early days? Actively seek opportunities to recreate some of that excitement and spontaneity. Communication is key here too. Don't be afraid to openly and honestly discuss your physical needs and desires with your partner.

This doesn't need to be a clinical session; it can be a playful and intimate conversation where you both express your desires and fantasies. Open dialogue is crucial for creating a shared sense of trust and comfort which ultimately leads to a higher degree of physical intimacy. It's about understanding each other's preferences and making adjustments that benefit both parties. Open communication creates a space for exploration and experimentation, fostering a relationship that's both fun and fulfilling.

Now, let's shift our focus to emotional intimacy, often the unsung hero of a successful relationship. This is the deeper connection, the vulnerability, the shared experiences and secrets. It's about feeling understood, accepted, and supported by your partner, regardless of your flaws or imperfections. This is the solid bedrock upon which a relationship can stand tall, even in the face of stormy weather.

Emotional intimacy isn't about constant agreement or never disagreeing. In fact, healthy disagreements are part of a healthy relationship. It's about being able to openly express your thoughts and feelings, even the difficult ones, without fear of judgment or criticism. It's about knowing you have a safe space to be yourself, without feeling pressured to conform to an unrealistic image. Think of it as a warm, cozy blanket, offering solace and comfort when life throws its curveballs.

Building emotional intimacy requires courage, a willingness to let your guard down and be truly vulnerable. It means sharing your fears, dreams, and insecurities with your partner, allowing them a glimpse into your inner world. This can be challenging, particularly if you've been hurt in the past. But the rewards far outweigh the risks. The feeling of being truly known and understood by another person is one of the deepest forms of connection and fulfillment imaginable.

How do you cultivate this type of intimacy? Start small. Share your daily experiences, even the mundane ones. Listen actively to your partner when they share their thoughts and feelings. Show genuine interest and empathy, even when you don't fully understand their perspective. It's like watering a delicate plant; consistent care and attention nurture its growth.

Regularly engage in activities that promote connection. Go for walks, have meaningful conversations, cook dinner together, read a book aloud to each other – activities that are deliberately designed to focus on shared experience. And set aside dedicated time for connection, even when life gets busy. If you're both feeling overwhelmed, take a step back and create a space for open and honest communication and understanding.

Regular acts of kindness also play a critical role in fostering emotional intimacy. These small gestures can be incredibly powerful in conveying your love and appreciation. They could range from leaving a loving note, making your partner's favorite coffee, or helping them with a task you know is challenging. These seemingly small gestures build a reservoir of appreciation and understanding within the relationship.

Sometimes, we mistakenly believe that emotional intimacy equates to constant, unyielding affection. This isn't true. Healthy relationships involve both highs and lows, moments of intense connection and times of quiet solitude. Respecting each other's need for personal space and independence is essential for fostering emotional intimacy, as this understanding strengthens trust and intimacy in the long run.

It's also important to acknowledge that building intimacy, both physical and emotional, takes time and effort. There will be moments of friction, misunderstandings, and even periods when the connection feels less strong. This is completely normal. It's like tending a garden – it requires consistent care and attention, even when the results aren't immediately visible. Persistence and patience are key ingredients in nurturing a thriving, intimate relationship.

What happens when the connection feels strained? It's important to address these issues proactively. Don't let problems fester and grow. Schedule a time to talk, express your concerns openly and honestly, and listen actively to your partner's perspective. If you're struggling to resolve the issues on your own, consider seeking professional help from a couple's therapist. They can provide a safe and neutral space for you to work through your challenges and develop healthy communication strategies. Think of them as relationship mechanics, adept at identifying and fixing the subtle glitches in the system.

The interplay between physical and emotional intimacy is complex and dynamic. They are interwoven, each supporting and strengthening the other. Strong emotional intimacy often leads to greater physical intimacy, and vice versa. Imagine them as two intertwined vines, growing stronger and more resilient together. Focus on nurturing both aspects, and you'll cultivate a relationship that is not only fulfilling but also deeply resilient. It's a journey, not a destination, and the rewards are worth every step of the way. The laughter, the shared experiences, the deep sense of belonging – these are the treasures that await those who invest in the ongoing cultivation of intimacy. So, nurture your vines, and watch your relationship flourish.

Maintaining Intimacy Over Time

Maintaining the vibrant tapestry of intimacy isn't a one-time achievement; it's a continuous act of creation, much like tending a garden. The initial bloom of passion is breathtaking, but the sustained beauty requires consistent nurturing, adaptation, and a healthy dose of understanding. Long-term relationships face unique challenges that can test the strength of even the most dedicated couples. The relentless march of time, the accumulation of shared experiences (both joyous and challenging), and the inevitable evolution of individual identities can all contribute to a gradual waning of intimacy. But fret not, this isn't a death knell; it's merely a call for recalibration.

One common pitfall is the insidious creep of *routine*. While establishing routine may be helpful to begin with, the daily grind, the predictable rhythms of work and household chores, can easily and quickly begin to overshadow the spontaneity and passion that characterized the early days of a relationship. Think of it like a well-worn path in a forest – it's comfortable, familiar, but it can also become monotonous. To combat this, couples need to consciously inject novelty and excitement into their lives. This doesn't require extravagant gestures or expensive trips; it's often the smaller, more intentional actions that make the biggest difference.

Consider the couple who, after twenty years of marriage, still dedicate a Friday night to a "date night," even if it's just pizza and a movie at home. The key is the dedicated time, free from distractions like work emails or household chores, solely focused on reconnecting. They may choose a different genre of film each week, introducing new elements into their shared experience. Another couple might take a weekly walk together, using the time to engage in deep conversation, share their thoughts and feelings, and simply enjoy each other's company. These seemingly simple acts maintain a sense of connection and intimacy amid busy lives.

Maintaining physical intimacy requires a conscious effort to prioritize physical touch and affection. This doesn't necessitate intense sexual encounters every night; rather, it involves incorporating small, meaningful gestures throughout the day. A gentle hand squeeze, a warm hug, a lingering kiss – these seemingly minor interactions communicate love and connection in powerful ways. Remember those early days of stolen kisses and lingering touches? Actively seek opportunities to recreate those moments of spontaneous affection, injecting a spark of excitement into your everyday interactions.

Open communication forms the bedrock of any successful long-term relationship, and this is particularly crucial when it comes to maintaining intimacy. This isn't about just discussing the mundane aspects of daily life; it's about creating a safe space for vulnerability and honest expression. Couples who successfully maintain intimacy over time prioritize regular check-ins, creating opportunities to discuss their emotional and physical needs. This might involve a dedicated "check-in" conversation once a week, or even a short daily conversation before bed, allowing each partner to share their feelings and concerns.

One couple I worked with, celebrating their 40th wedding anniversary, had implemented a "worry box" – a literal box where they would write down their anxieties and concerns. Once a week, they would empty the box and address the worries together, fostering a sense of shared vulnerability and support. This method, they said, helped prevent minor issues from escalating into major conflicts, preserving the emotional intimacy of their connection.

Adapting to life's inevitable changes is another crucial element in maintaining intimacy. Major life transitions, such as having children, changing careers, or dealing with the loss of loved ones, can significantly impact a couple's dynamic. These shifts can disrupt established routines and create new stressors that can test the resilience of a relationship. The key is to adapt and evolve together, maintaining open communication and a willingness to adjust as needed.

One couple I counseled had struggled to maintain their intimacy after the birth of their first child. Sleep deprivation, increased stress, and the overwhelming demands of parenthood left them feeling emotionally and physically exhausted.

Through therapy, they learned to prioritize dedicated "couple time," even if it was only for a short period each day, and to openly communicate their needs and frustrations. They also rediscovered the importance of shared activities, finding creative ways to incorporate their child into their shared time, creating a sense of unity as a family and preserving their couple connection. Their experience highlighted the importance of flexibility and a willingness to renegotiate the terms of their intimacy.

The misconception that intimacy is a static entity, a constant state of blissful connection, is a common stumbling block. Intimacy is dynamic, a fluid entity that ebbs and flows throughout the lifespan of a relationship. There will be times when the connection feels strong and vibrant, and other times when it feels more distant or strained. This is perfectly normal. The key is to approach these fluctuations with understanding and empathy, without labeling these periods of distance as "failure". Recognizing that the ebb and flow are part of a natural process can prevent feelings of guilt or self-recrimination. It's during these periods of distance that open communication, actively listening to your partner and expressing your own feelings without judgment, becomes essential.

Another essential component in maintaining intimacy is showing appreciation and expressing gratitude. In the busyness of daily life, it's easy to take our partners for granted, overlooking the small gestures and acts of kindness that sustain a relationship.

Consciously trying to express appreciation, whether it's through verbal affirmations, thoughtful gifts, or acts of service, can significantly enhance intimacy. The simple act of saying "thank you," and sincerely meaning it, can communicate a depth of appreciation that strengthens the emotional bond. Expressing gratitude doesn't require extravagant gestures; it's about recognizing and acknowledging the contributions your partner makes to your shared life.

Consider the couple who, after 30 years together, regularly leave each other short, loving notes expressing gratitude for something specific their partner had done. These notes, tucked into a pocket or left on a pillow, act as small reminders of love and appreciation, strengthening their emotional connection.

These seemingly insignificant acts contribute to the overall sense of being valued and cherished, essential for preserving intimacy over time. Maintaining intimacy in a long-term relationship is a continuous process of adaptation, communication, and mutual effort. It's about embracing the changes that life inevitably brings, while also cherishing the consistent acts of love and affection that build a strong foundation. It's a journey of rediscovering each other, even after years of familiarity, a journey that, when embarked upon with openness, understanding, and a playful spirit, can lead to an even deeper and more rewarding connection. The rewards of this sustained intimacy far outweigh the effort, leading to a rich and deeply fulfilling partnership that stands the test of time. The laughter, the shared memories, the unwavering support—these are the hallmarks of a relationship nurtured with consistent attention to the intricate dance of intimacy.

Seeking Couples Therapy

Sometimes, despite our best efforts, the garden of our relationship can become overgrown with weeds. Communication falters, resentment takes root, and the vibrant blooms of intimacy fade. When this happens, seeking professional help isn't a sign of weakness; it's a sign of strength, a testament to your commitment to nurturing your relationship. This is where couples therapy comes in. Think of couples therapy as a skilled gardener who can help you identify the problem weeds – those patterns of interaction, unresolved conflicts, or communication breakdowns – and then guide you in clearing them away, leaving room for healthy growth.

It's not about fixing one partner or blaming the other; it's about creating a shared understanding and developing strategies for a healthier, more fulfilling relationship. Many couples hesitate to seek therapy, often fueled by misconceptions and anxieties. Some worry about the stigma, fearing it signals a failing marriage. Others envision a dramatic confrontation in a therapist's office, reminiscent of a scene from a poorly written sitcom. Let me assure you, the reality is far more nuanced and often surprisingly helpful.

In my experience, successful couples therapy isn't about blame or judgment. It's a collaborative process, a safe space where you can openly discuss your feelings, concerns, and frustrations without the fear of immediate reprisal. A skilled therapist provides a neutral ground, guiding you toward understanding each other's perspectives, even when those perspectives are drastically different. They act as a facilitator, helping you navigate the complexities of communication and conflict resolution.

One of the most common concerns I hear is, "What if therapy reveals irreconcilable differences?" This is a valid concern, but it's important to remember that therapy isn't about forcing a relationship to work. Instead, it's about gaining clarity. Sometimes, therapy reveals that the relationship has run its course, and that separation is the most compassionate path forward. However, often, therapy helps couples find a deeper understanding of each other and a renewed commitment to the relationship.

So, how do you find the right therapist? Start by looking for someone specializing in couples therapy. Not all therapists are created equal, and a general therapist might not have the specialized skills needed to address the unique dynamics of a couple's relationship. You can search online directories of therapists, ask for referrals from your primary care physician or trusted friends, or even reach out to your insurance provider for a list of covered therapists.

When interviewing potential therapists, don't hesitate to ask questions. What is their approach to couple's therapy? What is their experience with couples facing similar challenges to yours? What is their approach to conflict resolution? Finding a good fit with a therapist is crucial, just like finding the right gardener for your garden. You need someone you feel comfortable and safe with, someone you trust to guide you through the process.

What can you expect in couples therapy? Expect to delve deep into your relationship dynamics. You'll likely discuss your communication patterns, conflict resolution styles, individual needs and expectations, and the underlying issues that contribute to any conflict. The therapist might use various techniques, from Cognitive Behavioral Therapy (CBT) to Emotionally Focused Therapy (EFT), depending on your specific needs and the nature of your challenges.

CBT focuses on identifying and changing negative thought patterns and behaviors that contribute to relationship problems. It's about learning to recognize and challenge unhelpful thought processes and replacing them with healthier, more positive ones. Imagine it like weeding out the negative self-talk and replacing it with self-compassion.

EFT, on the other hand, emphasizes emotional connection and understanding. It focuses on repairing attachment wounds and strengthening emotional bonds between partners. This approach helps you to access and express deeper emotions, improving empathy and understanding within the relationship. Think of it as nurturing the emotional soil of your relationship, allowing for deeper roots and stronger blossoms.

Remember, couples therapy isn't a quick fix. It's an ongoing process that requires commitment and effort from both partners. It's like tending a garden – it takes time, patience, and dedication to see results. There will be ups and downs, moments of breakthrough, and moments of frustration. But with the guidance of a skilled therapist, you'll gain valuable insights, learn new communication skills, and develop strategies to navigate future challenges together.

One of the most crucial elements in successful couples therapy is a willingness to actively participate. This means attending sessions regularly, completing any homework assignments the therapist provides, and honestly engaging in the process. It requires a shared commitment to making the relationship work. Think of it as both of you actively participating in the gardening process – one person can't do it alone.

Another vital ingredient is self-reflection. Couples therapy offers a unique opportunity for individual introspection, allowing you to examine your own role in the dynamics of the relationship. It's about understanding your own patterns, triggers, and contributions to both the positive and negative aspects of the partnership. This process isn't always easy; it may require facing uncomfortable truths and taking responsibility for your actions. But it is essential for fostering growth and understanding.

It's important to understand that couples therapy isn't a judgment on your relationship's worth; it's an investment in its potential. Many couples find it beneficial even when facing seemingly minor challenges, using it as a preventative measure to maintain a healthy connection. Think of it as regular check-ups for your relationship's health, ensuring it remains strong and vibrant.

Often, couples enter therapy feeling overwhelmed, stuck, and perhaps even hopeless. It's common to feel like you've tried everything, that nothing seems to work. But this is exactly why seeking professional help is so important. A skilled therapist can provide the guidance and support you need to break free from unhealthy patterns, build stronger communication skills, and rediscover the intimacy and connection that once defined your relationship.

Therapy isn't about fixing the other person; it's about understanding your own role in the relationship dynamic and learning how to communicate more effectively. It's about gaining new tools and techniques to navigate challenges and strengthen your bond. Consider couples therapy as an opportunity for growth, both individually and as a couple. It's a chance to deepen your understanding of yourselves and each other, strengthening the foundation of your relationship. It's a testament to your commitment to nurturing the love and connection you share. It's an investment in the future happiness and fulfillment of your relationship, akin to investing in the long-term health of your beautiful, albeit sometimes thorny, garden.

Remember, seeking help is a sign of strength, not weakness. It takes courage to acknowledge that you need support, and even more courage to actively seek it. By choosing to embark on this journey of self-discovery and relationship growth, you are investing in the long-term health and happiness of your partnership, strengthening the bonds of intimacy and fostering a more fulfilling and joyful life together. The journey might be challenging, but the rewards of a nurtured relationship far outweigh the effort. And remember, even the most experienced gardeners need a little help sometimes!

If there are problems in your relationships, your therapist won't tell you you're an asshole, but she'll see it, and so will you.

4. You're An Addict

Your therapist won't tell you you're an addict, although one of the most challenging struggles many people face is addiction.

The condition must be approached with a special type of grace and empathy from the helper, and more importantly, acknowledged by the recipient before the condition can even be addressed. Addiction isn't simply a matter of "lack of willpower," a simplistic explanation that often shames rather than helps. It's a complex interplay of biological, psychological, and social factors, a tangled web that needs careful unraveling.

We'll explore the widespread effects of common addictions, including substance use, gambling, and certain behaviors. While these categories aren't definitive and often overlap, they highlight the significant impact of addictive patterns.

Substance Addiction: This is perhaps the most understood form of addiction, encompassing the compulsive use of substances despite harmful consequences. These substances – from alcohol and nicotine to opioids, stimulants, and hallucinogens –hijack the brain's reward system, creating a powerful cycle of craving, use, and withdrawal. The consequences of substance addiction can be devastating.

Physically, the body takes a beating. Liver damage from alcohol abuse, lung cancer from smoking, and the myriad health problems associated with opioid use are just some examples. The impact on mental health is equally profound. Substance abuse can exacerbate existing mental health conditions like depression and anxiety, and in some cases, even trigger them. Beyond the physical and mental toll, substance addiction wreaks havoc on relationships. Trust is eroded, families are torn apart, and jobs are lost. The financial burden of addiction can be crippling, leading to debt, homelessness, and even legal trouble. The ripple effect extends outward, impacting not just the individual but also their loved ones, their community, and society. Think of it like a pebble dropped in a still pond – the initial impact is localized, but the ripples spread far and wide.

Consider the story of a friend's brother, Mark. Mark started with casual weekend drinking, a way to unwind after a stressful work week. Gradually, his drinking escalated. He started drinking during the week, hiding bottles around the house. His job was on the line; his marriage was crumbling. He eventually lost both. The addiction wasn't just affecting Mark; it had fractured his family, creating a deep chasm of pain and disappointment. It took years of struggle, multiple rehab attempts, and the unwavering support of his family for Mark to find his way back to a life of sobriety. His journey highlights the profound impact substance addiction has on an individual's life and the interconnected lives of those around him.

Gambling Addiction: Often overlooked, gambling addiction is a powerful and destructive force. The thrill of the win, the chase of the next big score, can quickly become a compulsive pursuit, leading to devastating financial losses, relationship breakdowns, and even criminal activity. Unlike substance addiction, the physical consequences of gambling addiction might not be as immediately apparent. However, the psychological and emotional toll is immense. The shame, the guilt, the constant worry about mounting debt can lead to depression, anxiety, and even suicidal thoughts. Families are often left financially ruined, emotionally drained, and deeply hurt. It's a form of addiction that feeds on hope, twisting it into a weapon of self-destruction.

The allure of gambling lies in the unpredictable nature of the outcome, the promise of a quick and easy win that can provide a momentary escape from the stresses of daily life. This illusion of control, however, quickly dissolves as the addiction takes hold, leaving the individual trapped in a cycle of loss and desperation.

Think of the plight of Sarah, a seemingly successful businesswoman who found solace in online poker after a difficult divorce. The initial wins fueled her addiction, but soon the losses mounted. She started borrowing money, lying to her friends and family, ultimately losing everything – her business, her home, and even her relationship with her children. Her story reveals the insidious nature of gambling addiction, how it can creep in unnoticed and consume everything in its path.

Behavioral Addictions: This broad category encompasses a range of compulsive behaviors, including internet addiction, sex addiction, shopping addiction, and even workaholism. These addictions don't involve substances, but they share the same underlying mechanism: a compulsive need for a particular behavior, despite negative consequences.

The impact of behavioral addictions can be just as devastating as substance or gambling addictions. Relationships suffer, productivity plummets, and mental health deteriorates. Financial ruin is a common consequence, particularly in cases of shopping addiction or impulsive spending fueled by other behavioral addictions. The isolation and shame associated with these addictions can be profoundly damaging. Often, individuals struggle in silence, ashamed to admit their struggles, leading to further isolation and despair.

Consider the case of David, a workaholic whose obsession with his job consumed his life. He neglected his family, his health, and even his own well-being in pursuit of professional success. He missed birthdays, anniversaries, and even his children's school events. His relentless pursuit of work came at a steep price—the erosion of his personal relationships and a profound sense of emptiness despite his professional achievements.

The common thread running through all types of addiction is the loss of control. The individual is no longer able to regulate their behavior, leading to a cycle of compulsive engagement and devastating consequences. Recovery is possible, but it requires acknowledging the problem, seeking professional help, and committing to a long-term process of change. This process involves developing healthier coping mechanisms, addressing underlying psychological issues, and building a strong support system.

The journey to recovery is not a linear one. There will be setbacks, moments of doubt, and even relapses. But with persistence, support, and the right kind of guidance, recovery is attainable. The key is understanding the underlying causes of the addiction, developing strategies to manage cravings and triggers, and learning healthier ways to cope with stress and difficult emotions. It's a journey that demands courage, compassion, and unwavering self-belief. It's a testament to the remarkable resilience of the human spirit, a demonstration of the power to heal and reclaim a life filled with purpose, meaning, and connection. Remember, seeking help is a sign of strength, not weakness. You are not alone, and there are people who care and want to support you on your path to recovery.

The Stages of Addiction and Recovery

The path to addiction, like a winding road, isn't a straight line to destruction. It's a gradual descent, often masked by seemingly harmless beginnings. Understanding the stages of addiction is crucial, not just for those struggling, but for loved ones seeking to support them. It helps us to understand the process, not to judge, but to empathize and provide effective help. Think of it like understanding the weather patterns before setting sail – knowing what to expect helps you navigate the storm.

The initial stage often involves experimentation or coping. It starts subtly – a glass of wine to unwind after work, a bet on a sports game for a bit of fun, or excessive hours at the office to achieve a feeling of accomplishment. In these early stages, the behavior isn't yet controlling; it's a means to an end—stress relief, excitement, a sense of accomplishment. The individual might not even recognize the potential for harm. It's like tasting a single piece of cake –initially enjoyable, but far from a full-blown indulgence.

As the behavior continues, the need to engage increases. What began as an occasional indulgence transforms into a regular habit. The frequency and intensity escalate. The glass of wine becomes two; the casual bet becomes a daily ritual; the extra hours at work extend into evenings and weekends. This is where the slippery slope begins. The rewards become shorter-lived and the consequences, though present, are often minimized or ignored. This is analogous to slowly increasing your cake intake – one piece a day soon becomes two, and the feeling of guilt, initially present, fades into the background as you chase that fleeting pleasure. This might be accompanied by denial, rationalization, and attempts to downplay the severity of the habit. The escalation continues until the behavior becomes compulsive. Now, the need to engage overrides any rational thought.

Consequences are ignored or actively minimized. The individual may try to quit but finds themselves unable to resist the urge. Their life revolves around addictive behavior, and relationships, work, and other aspects of their life suffer significantly. This phase is marked by a profound loss of control. This is like finding yourself in a situation where you have eaten the entire cake and then some –the initial pleasure is long gone, but the compulsion to eat has taken over, despite the clear negative consequences. This is a critical stage where intervention is crucial. The individual's struggle is no longer just about willpower; it's a battle against a powerful compulsion. At this stage, the individual may feel trapped, ashamed, and alone.

In many cases, physical and psychological dependence sets in. This is particularly evident in substance addictions, where the body develops a tolerance to the substance, requiring increasing amounts to achieve the same effect. Withdrawal symptoms – physical and psychological discomfort that occurs when the substance is not used– can be intense and even life-threatening. This is the point where the cake is no longer just about the taste but a physical addiction. The cravings, the shaking, the emotional turmoil are all signs that the body is physically dependent. It's not just about the mind anymore; the body is now actively crying out for the addictive substance.

Even behavioral addictions can lead to forms of dependence, such as withdrawal symptoms manifesting as anxiety, irritability, and difficulty concentrating when the behavior is restricted. This intense dependency highlights the powerful hold that the addiction has on the brain and body. The recovery process, in its simplest form, reverses these stages. However, it's rarely a simple, linear progression. Instead, it's often a cyclical process with setbacks and relapses. The journey isn't a race, but a marathon. The initial step is acknowledging the problem. This can be one of the most difficult hurdles, as denial and shame often prevent individuals from facing the truth. Seeking help – whether from family, friends, or professionals – is vital. This creates a support system that provides encouragement and accountability. Professional guidance helps to develop coping mechanisms and address underlying psychological issues that may have contributed to the addiction. This is like finding a skilled baker who can help create healthy alternatives, reducing the cravings and offering support for the journey towards a healthier relationship with food.

The next stage involves detox, if necessary. For substance addictions, this is often medically supervised to manage withdrawal symptoms. For behavioral addictions, detox involves gradually reducing or eliminating the problematic behavior. This might involve seeking professional help, such as therapy or support groups. This is like gradually reducing the amount of cake you eat each day until the cravings eventually subside.

Rehabilitation and therapy play a significant role in the recovery process. These interventions help individuals identify triggers, develop healthier coping mechanisms, address underlying psychological issues, and build a strong support system. It's about restructuring the brain to cope with life's challenges in healthier ways, breaking the cycle of reliance on addictive behavior. Think of it like learning new recipes, new ways to bake, or entirely different culinary paths that offer just as much (or even more) satisfaction than the addictive cake.

Relapse is a common part of recovery. It's not a sign of failure, but an opportunity to learn and adjust strategies. It's crucial to avoid self-blame and focus on identifying the triggers that led to the relapse and develop more effective coping strategies. View each relapse as a learning experience, not a judgment on your character. This is like accidentally taking a bite of cake, but recognizing it, understanding the impulse, and choosing a healthier alternative next time.

Long-term recovery involves continuous effort and commitment. It requires ongoing maintenance, self-care, and support from others. Regular check-ups, therapy sessions, and participation in support groups are vital for ongoing success. This is like maintaining a healthy lifestyle: a commitment to regular exercise, proper nutrition, and mindful eating, so that the cravings for cake never get the upper hand.

The journey to recovery is a deeply personal one, a testament to the resilience of the human spirit. It requires courage, self-compassion, and unwavering support. It's a process of rebuilding one's life, one day at a time, learning to manage triggers, cravings, and vulnerabilities in a healthier, more sustainable way. It's a journey of rediscovery, leading to a life filled with purpose, meaning, and connection, free from the grip of addiction. And remember, you are not alone in this journey. There are resources available, people who understand, and a community ready to support you every step of the way. The road to recovery may be long and winding, but the destination – a healthier, happier you – are well worth the effort.

Treatment Options for Addiction
One of the first steps, particularly for substance addiction, often involves detoxification, or detox. Think of detox as the initial spring cleaning of your body, ridding it of the substance that's been holding it hostage. This process can be incredibly challenging, as your body adjusts to the absence of the substance. Withdrawal symptoms can range from mild discomfort to severe, even life-threatening complications, depending on the substance and the severity of the addiction. This is why medically supervised detox is often recommended. Under the care of medical professionals, the withdrawal process is managed safely and comfortably,

minimizing the risks of complications and providing support during this vulnerable period.

Medically supervised detox isn't just about managing withdrawal symptoms; it also provides a structured environment, ensuring the individual's safety and well-being. This is crucial, as individuals undergoing detox often experience intense cravings, emotional instability, and physical discomfort. A safe and supportive environment helps minimize these challenges and sets a strong foundation for the next stage of recovery. Imagine detox as the first leg of a marathon – you might be exhausted and sore, but you've successfully completed the most challenging part of the journey and are ready to move forward with a stronger sense of purpose.

Beyond detox, therapy is arguably the cornerstone of successful addiction treatment. This isn't your typical "lie on the couch and talk" therapy, though that can be a part of it. Effective therapy for addiction is active, engaging, and often tailored to specific approaches. Cognitive Behavioral Therapy (CBT) is a common and very effective technique. It focuses on identifying and changing negative thought patterns and behaviors that contribute to addiction. Think of it as retraining your brain – rewiring it to respond to triggers and cravings in a healthier way.

For instance, if someone is struggling with alcohol addiction, CBT might help them identify situations that trigger their urge to drink, such as stress or social gatherings. Then, the therapy works to develop healthier coping mechanisms to deal with those triggers without resorting to alcohol. This might involve practicing relaxation techniques, building a stronger support system, or developing healthier ways to socialize. The goal is to help individuals break the cycle of negative thinking and self-destructive behaviors, building a more positive and resilient approach to life.

Another powerful therapeutic approach is Dialectical Behavior Therapy (DBT). DBT is particularly effective for individuals who struggle with emotional regulation, self-harm, or impulsive behaviors, often associated with addiction. It teaches skills in mindfulness, distress tolerance, emotional regulation, and interpersonal effectiveness. These skills help individuals manage intense emotions, cope with difficult situations, and build healthier relationships.

Imagine DBT as a toolbox filled with practical strategies for navigating life's challenges. These skills empower individuals to handle stress, cope with cravings, and avoid impulsive behaviors that could lead to relapse. This is a crucial aspect of recovery because it equips individuals with the tools they need to manage the long-term challenges of staying sober or free from addictive behaviors. DBT helps them to become their own best therapists, equipped to face whatever life throws their way.

Furthermore, family therapy can play a crucial role in the recovery process. Addiction doesn't exist in a vacuum; it impacts the entire family system. Family therapy provides a safe space for family members to address their feelings, improve communication, and work towards healing together. This can be incredibly beneficial in rebuilding trust and fostering a supportive environment that is essential for long-term recovery.

Support groups, like Alcoholics Anonymous (AA) or Narcotics Anonymous (NA), provide a vital source of support and community. These groups offer a safe and non-judgmental space where individuals can share their experiences, learn from others, and receive ongoing support. The power of shared experience and mutual understanding is invaluable, especially during challenging times. Imagine it as a network of fellow hikers, each supporting the other as they navigate the challenging terrain of recovery.

Medication-assisted treatment (MAT) is another important option for certain types of addiction, particularly opioid and alcohol addiction. MAT involves using medication to manage withdrawal symptoms, reduce cravings, and prevent relapse. It's not a standalone solution but a valuable tool when used in conjunction with other therapies like CBT or DBT. For instance, methadone or buprenorphine can be used to treat opioid addiction by reducing cravings and withdrawal symptoms, allowing individuals to focus on other aspects of their recovery. Similar medications are available for alcohol addiction, helping to reduce cravings and prevent relapse. It is crucial to understand that MAT is not a replacement for therapy or support groups; instead, it's a valuable tool that can significantly improve the chances of success when combined with other elements of a comprehensive treatment plan.

The choice of treatment is highly individual, depending on the type of addiction, its severity, the individual's personal circumstances, and their preferences. There's no one-size-fits-all approach, and it's often beneficial to explore a combination of these modalities. A skilled therapist or addiction specialist can help you create a personalized treatment plan that addresses your unique needs and challenges. They can guide you through the options, helping you choose the path that best suits your individual journey.

Beyond the formal treatments, self-care plays a crucial role in maintaining long-term recovery. This includes prioritizing physical health through regular exercise, nutritious diet, and sufficient sleep. It also involves nurturing mental and emotional well-being through mindfulness practices like meditation or yoga, engaging in hobbies, and cultivating positive social connections.

Imagine self-care as regular maintenance for your vehicle. Just as you wouldn't neglect routine oil changes and tire rotations, neglecting self-care can lead to setbacks in recovery. Prioritizing self-care is not selfish; it's essential for maintaining both physical and mental resilience, enabling you to navigate the challenges of recovery with increased strength and confidence.

Relapse can be a part of the recovery process. It's not a sign of failure, but an opportunity to learn and adjust your strategy. If a relapse occurs, it's essential to avoid self-blame and focus on understanding what triggered the relapse and developing more effective coping strategies. Seek support from your therapist, support groups, or loved ones, and don't be afraid to adjust your treatment plan as needed. Relapse is a bump in the road, not a detour from your destination.

Recovery is a continuous journey that requires ongoing effort, self-compassion, and unwavering support. But it is a journey worth taking – a journey towards a healthier, happier, and more fulfilling life, free from the grip of addiction.

Remember, you are not alone.

There are resources available, people who understand, and a community waiting to support you every step of the way. This is your journey, your path to recovery, and you have the strength and resilience to overcome this challenge. Take it one step at a time, celebrate your victories, and know that a brighter future is within reach.

Relapse Prevention Strategies
Relapse is, unfortunately, a common experience for many individuals navigating the path to recovery from addiction. It's not a sign of weakness or failure; it's often a part of the learning process. Think of it like learning to ride a bike – you're bound to fall

a few times before you find your balance. The key is to learn from those falls, get back on the bike, and keep practicing. The same principle applies to addiction recovery.

One of the most effective relapse prevention strategies is identifying your personal triggers. Triggers are those specific situations, people, places, or feelings that increase your cravings or urges to use the substance or engage in addictive behavior. These triggers can be surprisingly subtle and varied. For example, a specific song, a particular smell, a certain type of conversation, or even a particular emotional state can act as a powerful trigger.

Identifying these triggers requires honest self-reflection and perhaps some journaling. Consider keeping a daily log where you note down situations, feelings, or thoughts that lead to increased cravings. This log can help you pinpoint specific patterns and vulnerabilities. Let's say, for instance, that you notice you tend to crave alcohol when feeling stressed after work. That's your trigger: stress after work. Now that you've identified it, you can begin to develop strategies to address that specific stress.

Building a strong support system is another crucial element of relapse prevention. This isn't just about having friends and family; it's about having individuals who understand your journey and can offer consistent, supportive guidance. This could include a therapist, support group members, sponsors, or trusted friends and family members. It's important to choose individuals who provide unconditional positive regard, and who can offer support without judgment, even during moments of vulnerability or relapse. These individuals act as a safety net, a source of strength when you need it most.

Having a readily available plan for coping with cravings or urges is essential. When a craving hits, you need a well-rehearsed strategy to counter it, something you can implement immediately. This could involve deep breathing exercises, mindfulness meditation, engaging in a planned distraction (like a workout, a walk, or calling a friend), or reaching out to your support system. The key is to have a toolbox of techniques readily available, so you don't fall back on your old habits when faced with an intense craving.

Developing healthy coping mechanisms is fundamental to long-term recovery. Addiction often serves as a coping mechanism for underlying emotional pain or stress. Without addressing the root causes of the addiction, the chances of relapse significantly increase. Therapy can help you develop healthier ways to manage stress, anxiety, depression, or trauma. This might involve learning relaxation techniques, improving communication skills, or developing healthier ways to express your emotions.

Take the example of someone who uses drugs to cope with loneliness. Therapy might help them understand the root of their loneliness, develop strategies for building healthier relationships, and engage in activities that foster a sense of connection and belonging. This shifts the focus from using substances as a coping mechanism to actively addressing and overcoming the underlying emotional issues. This is an active, not passive approach to recovery.

Regular self-care is often overlooked but plays a surprisingly significant role in preventing relapse. This is not about pampering; it's about nurturing your physical, mental, and emotional well-being. Prioritize regular exercise, a balanced diet, sufficient sleep, and engaging in activities you enjoy. Regular self-care boosts your resilience, providing you with the strength to withstand stressful situations or cravings that might otherwise trigger a relapse. Think of it as strengthening your immune system – a stronger you is better equipped to fight off the urge to relapse.

Seek support from your therapist, support group, or trusted loved ones. Don't hesitate to share your experience openly and honestly. This is precisely why these support systems are in place – to provide a safe space for you to navigate challenges like relapse. Don't isolate yourself; isolation can exacerbate feelings of guilt and shame, increasing the risk of further relapse. Consider this analogy: Imagine you're building a house. You might encounter setbacks during construction – a storm might damage part of the structure, or you might discover a flaw in the foundation. You wouldn't tear down the entire house; you'd repair the damage, adjust your plans, and continue building. Relapse is similar; it's an opportunity to identify and fix the flaws in your recovery plan, and then continue building a stronger, healthier life.

Many find that incorporating mindfulness practices into their relapse prevention plan is invaluable. Mindfulness helps you develop an increased awareness of your thoughts, feelings, and bodily sensations without judgment. This heightened awareness can help you identify early warning signs of a potential relapse, such as increased stress, anxiety, or cravings. By noticing these signs early, you can proactively implement your coping strategies before they escalate into a full-blown relapse.

Imagine mindfulness as a way to see what's coming, like a warning system. It helps you observe difficult feelings without being controlled by them, so you can choose how to react instead of just reacting. This gives you time to use your coping tools before a craving becomes too strong.

Furthermore, it's essential to regularly evaluate your relapse prevention plan. This isn't a static document; it's a living, breathing tool that needs to adapt to your changing needs and circumstances. Regularly review your triggers, coping mechanisms, and support systems. Are they still effective? Do you need to add anything? Do you need to adjust anything based on your recent experiences? This ongoing evaluation ensures that your relapse prevention plan remains a relevant and effective guide on your journey to recovery.

Regular check-ins with your therapist or support group can be exceptionally beneficial. They can provide an objective perspective, helping you identify potential blind spots or areas needing improvement in your plan. They can offer guidance, support, and encouragement, reinforcing your commitment to recovery. They're there to cheer you on, providing support when you need it most.

Remember, this isn't a solo mission; you have a team supporting your journey.

Finally, remember that recovery is a journey, not a destination. There will be ups and downs, successes and setbacks. Embrace the challenges, learn from your mistakes, and celebrate your victories. Be patient with yourself, offer yourself compassion, and remember that you are not alone. There are resources available, people who understand, and a community waiting to support you every step of the way. Your journey to recovery is worth it; a brighter, healthier future awaits.

Support Systems and Resources for Addiction

Building a robust support system is crucial in the fight against addiction. You need a strong team supporting you every step of the way.

This support system extends far beyond just friends and family, though their love and encouragement are invaluable. Consider it a multi-faceted approach: a network of support that provides different types of assistance at different times. Some days you might need the practical help of a friend bringing you groceries, other days you might need the deep emotional support of a therapist, and still others might require the shared experience and camaraderie of a support group.

Let's talk about the different types of support you might find helpful. First, there's professional support. A therapist specializing in addiction is an invaluable resource. They provide a safe and confidential space for you to explore the underlying causes of your addiction, develop coping mechanisms, and work through any emotional or psychological issues contributing to your substance use. Therapists can also help you identify and manage triggers, preventing relapse. Don't hesitate to seek a therapist – it's a sign of strength, not weakness.

Support groups, such as Alcoholics Anonymous (AA), Narcotics Anonymous (NA), and others tailored to specific addictions, offer a powerful sense of community and shared experience. Hearing from others who have walked a similar path, who understand the challenges and triumphs of recovery, is incredibly validating and empowering. These groups provide a safe space to share your struggles without judgment, receive encouragement, and learn from others' experiences. The power of shared experience should not be underestimated.

Then there are 12-step programs, which provide a structured framework for recovery through a series of steps focused on self-reflection, amends-making, and spiritual growth. Many find these programs immensely helpful in building a foundation for lasting sobriety. While not for everyone, the structured nature of these programs offers a roadmap for many.

Beyond professional and group support, your personal network of friends and family plays a vital role. It's important, however, to carefully cultivate these relationships, setting clear boundaries and expectations. Make sure those close to you understand the commitment you've made to your recovery and how they can best support you. This might mean asking for their help in avoiding triggering situations or simply having someone to talk to when you're feeling overwhelmed.

However, it's crucial to remember that not all support is created equal. While well-meaning, some friends and family might unintentionally undermine your efforts, perhaps by enabling your addiction or offering unsolicited advice. Learn to identify those relationships that are truly supportive and those that aren't. It's okay to limit contact with individuals who aren't contributing positively to your recovery.

Remember, you deserve support that is unconditional, non-judgmental, and consistently encouraging. If someone is constantly belittling your efforts or making you feel worse about yourself, it might be time to reassess that relationship. Your emotional well-being during recovery is paramount, and you deserve to surround yourself with people who genuinely support your journey.

Now, let's move beyond personal support systems and talk about the wealth of resources available. There are countless organizations dedicated to helping individuals and families struggling with addiction. These organizations offer a range of services, from crisis hotlines and treatment referrals to educational materials and support groups.

Websites such as the Substance Abuse and Mental Health Services Administration (SAMHSA) website provide extensive information on addiction, treatment options, and available resources. SAMHSA's National Helpline is a 24/7, 365-day-a-year, confidential free service that provides referrals to local treatment facilities, support groups, and community-based organizations. They're a fantastic resource.

Many local communities also offer free or low-cost addiction treatment services, including counseling, medication-assisted treatment (MAT), and support groups. Checking with your local health department or searching online for addiction services in your area can connect you with these essential resources.

For families and loved ones of individuals with addiction, there are numerous organizations and support groups available. These groups offer education, guidance, and support to help families navigate the challenges of dealing with addiction within their families. They provide a safe space to share experiences, learn coping strategies, and find strength in community.

Remember, seeking help is not a sign of weakness, it's a sign of strength. It takes courage to admit you need help, and even more courage to actively seek it. Don't hesitate to reach out to any of the resources mentioned here or to seek help from your doctor or another healthcare provider. There are people who care and resources available to help you navigate your journey to recovery.

One particularly important aspect of your support system is the role of a sponsor or mentor. In 12-step programs, sponsors provide guidance, support, and accountability. They've walked the walk, so they understand the unique challenges you're facing. They offer a listening ear, provide encouragement, and help you stay on track with your recovery goals.

Beyond the formal structures of support groups and 12-step programs, consider the power of informal support. This might involve developing close relationships with trusted friends, colleagues, or members of your faith community. These individuals can provide crucial emotional support, helping you celebrate your successes and navigate difficult times.

Building a solid support network takes time and effort. It's not a passive process; it's active cultivation. It requires reaching out, building relationships, and consistently engaging with your support system. But the investment is invaluable. A strong support system provides the safety net, encouragement, and practical assistance you need to navigate the challenges of addiction recovery.

Moreover, remember that your support system is not static. It evolves as you progress on your recovery journey. What works for you in the early stages might not be as effective later. It's okay to adjust your support network as your needs change. Perhaps you find that group therapy becomes more beneficial than individual therapy as you progress. Or you might find that certain relationships provide more support than others at different stages of your journey.

Remember to be proactive in your approach to building and maintaining your support system. Don't wait until you're in crisis to reach out. Regularly check in with your support network, share your progress, and let them know what you need. Building strong relationships takes time, but the rewards are immeasurable.

Finally, let's circle back to the idea of relapse. Even with the strongest support system in place, relapse can occur. The crucial thing is to remember that relapse is not a failure; it's a setback. Your support system is there to help you navigate these setbacks, to offer you compassion, and to help you get back on track. Don't be afraid to lean on your support system when you need it most. They're there to help you up, dust yourself off, and keep moving forward on your path to recovery.

Your therapist might not tell you that you are an addict, but she can offer a guiding light to find your path to recovery.

5. Your Hygiene Is Horrendous

Your therapist won't tell you your hygiene is horrendous. But if it is, she's struggling not to tell you.

While it might seem trivial compared to the emotional and psychological battles you face, the connection between hygiene and self-esteem is surprisingly profound. Neglecting personal care can subtly, yet powerfully, undermine your progress and recovery.

Think of it this way: you're building a beautiful house (your life), meticulously laying the foundation (support system, therapy, etc.), and carefully crafting each room (developing coping mechanisms, achieving milestones). But what if you left the house unkempt, littered with trash, and filled with unpleasant odors? Would you feel proud of your accomplishments? Would you invite guests? Likely not. Your external environment mirrors your internal state. Maintaining good hygiene is about taking care of the "house" you inhabit – your body – and demonstrating respect for yourself in the process.

Neglecting hygiene isn't simply about looking presentable; it's about self-respect and self-worth. When you feel good physically, it often translates into feeling better emotionally. It's a ripple effect. A simple shower, a clean shave, or freshly washed clothes can have a surprising impact on your mood and self-confidence. It's a small act of self-care that can have big repercussions.

Let's examine the link between poor hygiene and decreased self-esteem. When you feel unclean or unkempt, it can trigger negative self-perception. You might start feeling self-conscious, avoiding social interactions, and withdrawing from activities you once enjoyed. This isolation can further exacerbate feelings of worthlessness and depression, potentially hindering your progress in recovery. This cycle of neglect, self-doubt, and further withdrawal is a trap to be avoided.

Imagine a scenario where someone is struggling with addiction and also neglecting basic hygiene. They might feel too overwhelmed to shower, change clothes, or brush their teeth. This lack of self-care creates a negative feedback loop. They feel bad about themselves, which leads to further neglect, which in turn worsens their self-image. This can significantly impact their motivation to engage in recovery efforts. It becomes a heavy burden to carry alongside their other challenges.

The effects extend beyond personal feelings. Poor hygiene can also impact your social interactions. People are more likely to distance themselves from someone who constantly smells unpleasant or appears unkempt. This social isolation can be incredibly damaging, especially during the recovery process where connection and support are vital. You are actively pushing away the very people who could be helping you climb out of the pit.

Consider a specific example: someone attends a support group meeting, but their appearance and hygiene are poor. They might feel ashamed and embarrassed, leading to reluctance to participate fully. This reluctance can prevent them from connecting with others, sharing their experiences, and benefiting from the support offered within the group. They are potentially missing out on crucial connections simply because of their hygiene habits.

The impact on relationships with family and friends can be similarly significant. While loved ones might be understanding and supportive, consistent neglect of personal hygiene can still create a sense of distance or discomfort. It's not about judgment; it's about the practical implications of poor hygiene. It's difficult to maintain close, healthy relationships when basic hygiene is neglected.

Think about breaking down the hygiene routine into manageable chunks. Instead of feeling overwhelmed by the thought of a full shower, focus on washing your face and hands. If changing your clothes feels like too much effort, start with changing your shirt. Small victories contribute to a larger sense of accomplishment and boost your self-esteem.

Beyond the physical act of cleaning, consider incorporating some elements of self-pampering into your hygiene routine. Choose a body wash with a scent you enjoy, use a luxurious moisturizer, or listen to calming music while showering. Transforming this necessary chore into a small act of self-care can elevate the experience and make it more enjoyable.

Remember that neglecting hygiene is often a symptom of a larger issue, whether it's depression, fatigue, or simply a lack of motivation. Addressing the underlying causes is just as important as addressing the hygiene itself. It's crucial to approach hygiene as an integral part of your overall self-care strategy. It's not a superficial act, but a fundamental component of self-respect and recovery.

Consider seeking professional support if hygiene is a significant struggle. A therapist can help you understand the underlying reasons for neglecting self-care and develop strategies for overcoming those challenges. They can provide coping mechanisms to help you manage feelings of overwhelmingness and to prioritize your well-being. Remember, it's okay to ask for help – it's a sign of strength, not weakness.

Moreover, your support system plays a significant role in encouraging and maintaining good hygiene. Consider communicating your struggles openly with your support network and asking for their encouragement and support in establishing a regular hygiene routine. They might be able to help you with reminders or even offer practical assistance. Building a support system that extends to the daily aspects of life can be incredibly empowering. Finally, remember that improvement is progress. Don't beat yourself up over setbacks or lapses. If you miss a shower one day, don't let it derail your efforts. Simply get back on track the next day.

Consistency, not perfection, is the key to establishing lasting healthy hygiene habits. Celebrate the small wins – each shower, each clean set of clothes – as milestones in your recovery journey. They are all steps in the right direction, strengthening your self-esteem and reinforcing your commitment to a healthier, happier you. You are worth it.

Mental Health and Hygiene Practices

Let's delve deeper into the fascinating and often overlooked connection between our mental health and our hygiene practices. It's not just about looking presentable; it's about a powerful, often subconscious, feedback loop between how we care for our bodies and how we feel about ourselves. Think of it as a mirror reflecting our inner world onto our outer appearance. When our mental health struggles, our hygiene routines often suffer, and vice versa.

This isn't about judgment; it's about understanding a complex relationship.

Consider someone grappling with depression. The simple act of showering might feel insurmountable. The energy required, the perceived effort, can feel like climbing a mountain when already weighed down by emotional burdens. The very idea of caring for their physical appearance might seem frivolous or pointless when their inner world feels desolate. This isn't laziness; it's a manifestation of their illness. The motivation is simply absent. This lack of self-care then further fuels feelings of negativity, leading to a vicious cycle of decline.

This isn't limited to depression. Anxiety can also significantly disrupt hygiene routines. The overwhelming feeling of needing to be "perfect" can lead to paralysis. The individual might spend hours agonizing over the smallest details, leading to a procrastination cycle that prevents them from starting their hygiene routine at all. Or the fear of judgment—from others, or even themselves—can be so overwhelming that they avoid personal grooming altogether. The result is the same: a lack of self-care which exacerbates the mental health condition.

Furthermore, conditions like bipolar disorder can lead to erratic hygiene practices, fluctuating between periods of meticulous grooming and complete neglect, reflecting the intense mood swings characteristic of the condition. During manic episodes, individuals may have the energy for excessive self-care, while depressive episodes can lead to complete neglect. This inconsistency can be extremely challenging to manage, both for the individual and their loved ones.

But it's not only mental illness; other life stressors can also take their toll. Burnout, chronic pain, grief – all of these significantly impact our energy levels and motivation, making even basic hygiene tasks feel like herculean efforts. When we're exhausted and depleted, self-care often falls by the wayside. We're not intentionally neglecting ourselves, but rather simply unable to muster the effort.

However, the beauty of this connection lies in its reciprocal nature. Just as poor mental health can impact hygiene, so too can improving our hygiene have a surprisingly significant positive effect on our mental state. The act of showering, for example, can be surprisingly therapeutic. The warm water, the feeling of cleansing, can be incredibly soothing. It's a small act of self-compassion, a silent acknowledgment of our worthiness.

Think about the sensory experience of washing your hair with a fragrant shampoo, the feeling of clean, fresh skin after a shower, or the subtle confidence boost that comes with freshly ironed clothes. These seemingly minor details contribute to a cumulative effect. The improved physical sensation translates into a feeling of control and self-respect. It's a tangible reminder of our capacity to care for ourselves.

The benefits go beyond the purely sensory. Improving our hygiene can also improve our social interactions. When we feel clean and presentable, we're more likely to engage socially, to participate in activities, to connect with others. This increased social engagement can significantly improve our mood, bolstering our sense of belonging and combating feelings of isolation and loneliness. Moreover, maintaining a regular hygiene routine is an act of self-discipline, and the accomplishment of completing these tasks, no matter how small, builds self-esteem. Each time we successfully overcome the inertia and complete a task; we strengthen our belief in our own capabilities. It's a simple yet potent method for reinforcing positive self-talk.

It's not about striving for unrealistic standards of perfection.

Recovery and self-care aren't about flawless execution; they're about progress. Some days will be easier than others. There will be days when even the simplest tasks feel monumental. The key is to focus on small, manageable steps, setting realistic goals and celebrating every small victory. Start with one thing: brushing your teeth twice a day. Then add another: washing your face. Gradually build up a routine that is sustainable and manageable, focusing on consistency rather than perfection. Remember, progress, however incremental, is still progress. Consider making your hygiene routine more enjoyable. Choose products that you enjoy, create a relaxing environment, perhaps listening to calming music while showering, or using aromatherapy products. Transforming this essential task from a chore into a moment of self-indulgence can make all the difference.

Ultimately, addressing poor hygiene requires a holistic approach. It's about attending to both the physical and the mental. If hygiene is a significant challenge, it's crucial to seek professional help. A therapist or counselor can provide guidance and support, helping you address any underlying mental health conditions contributing to the issue. They can help you develop strategies to manage your symptoms and improve your self-care practices.

Don't hesitate to reach out for help. It's a sign of strength, not weakness, to acknowledge when we need support and to actively seek it. Remember, you deserve to feel good, both inside and out. Caring for your physical hygiene is an act of self-respect, a vital step in nurturing your overall well-being. It's an investment in yourself, a journey of self-compassion. And that journey, however challenging at times, is entirely worth taking.

Practical Hygiene Tips for Improved Wellbeing

Let's translate that abstract concept of improved hygiene into concrete, actionable steps. We're not aiming for perfection here—that's a recipe for burnout and self-criticism, two things we definitely want to avoid. Instead, we're focusing on building sustainable habits, small wins that accumulate into significant positive change. Think of it like building muscle; you don't go from zero to marathon runner overnight. You start with small, manageable workouts and gradually increase intensity and duration. Hygiene is the same.

Start with the basics. Let's talk showering. For many struggling with mental health challenges, the very idea of showering can feel overwhelming. But let's break it down. It doesn't have to be a long, luxurious affair. A quick five-minute shower can be incredibly refreshing and revitalizing. Focus on the sensory experience: the warmth of the water on your skin, the invigorating feeling of cleanliness. If a full shower feels too daunting, start with a quick washcloth cleanse – just get your face, underarms, and groin area clean. That's a win, a step towards better hygiene, even if it's not a full-blown shower.

Think about making it more enjoyable. Experiment with different shower gels or soaps – find a scent that appeals to you, something uplifting or calming. Play some relaxing music; create a small sanctuary for yourself during those few minutes. Turn the shower into a mini-spa experience, a little slice of self-care in your day. The goal isn't just to get clean; it's to make it an experience you look forward to, even if just a little.

Next, let's tackle oral hygiene. Brushing your teeth twice a day might seem trivial, but it's a crucial element of overall hygiene and well-being. Bad breath can lead to social isolation and self-consciousness, exacerbating feelings of low self-esteem. Make it a routine: brush your teeth first thing in the morning and right before bed. Keep your toothbrush readily accessible and consider using a timer to ensure you brush for at least two minutes. Experiment with different toothpastes until you find one that you like; the right flavor can motivate you to brush more often.

Handwashing is another often overlooked yet critically important hygiene practice. We're constantly touching surfaces teeming with germs, and proper handwashing is a simple, effective way to

reduce your risk of illness. It also has a psychological benefit; the act of cleansing your hands can be surprisingly symbolic, a way to metaphorically wash away stress or negative feelings. Make it a habit to wash your hands thoroughly with soap and water after using the restroom, before meals, and after touching public
Surfaces.

Beyond showering and oral hygiene, consider grooming. This can encompass anything from combing your hair to trimming your nails. Again, we're not aiming for perfection; we're aiming for progress. A quick comb through your hair can make you feel instantly more put-together. Trimming your nails prevents them from becoming ragged and unhealthy, and it's a small act of self-care you can easily integrate into your daily routine.
For individuals struggling with severe mental health challenges, these simple tasks can feel monumental. Remember, small steps are still steps. Start with one thing, maybe just brushing your teeth, and build from there. Don't beat yourself up on days when you fall short; acknowledge it, forgive

yourself, and try again tomorrow. The key is consistency, not perfection.

To make this easier, try establishing a daily routine. Write it down, if it helps. It could look something like this:

Morning: Brush teeth, wash face, get dressed.
Evening: Brush teeth, wash face, change into pajamas.

This is just a basic framework; adjust it to fit your individual needs and preferences. Remember, the point isn't to create a rigid, inflexible schedule; it's to create a structure that supports your well-being. And don't forget to build in some flexibility. Life happens, and some days will inevitably be more challenging than others. That's okay.

Another helpful tactic is to incorporate these hygiene practices into existing routines. For instance, you could brush your teeth while you listen to the news in the morning or put on some music while you shower. Connecting hygiene routines to already established habits can make them feel less like chores and more like integrated parts of your day.

Let's talk about laundry. Clean clothes can significantly impact your mood and self-esteem. The feeling of wearing clean, freshly laundered clothes is a subtle but powerful boost to your confidence. If doing a full load of laundry seems daunting, start small. Wash just one or two items. It's still a step in the right direction, a small victory to celebrate. Consider using laundry detergent with a pleasant scent; the fragrance can add a little joy to your routine.

Remember that a capsule laundry detergent can simplify this task even further. Consider the power of scent. Aromatherapy can be a surprisingly effective tool in managing stress and anxiety. Lavender, chamomile, and sandalwood are all known for their calming properties.

Consider adding a few drops of essential oil to your bath or shower gel or using an aromatherapy diffuser in your bathroom. This can transform a simple hygiene routine into a mini-spa experience, enhancing both its physical and psychological benefits.

Furthermore, remember that your environment plays a significant role in your hygiene habits. A cluttered, disorganized bathroom can make it even harder to maintain a regular hygiene routine. Take a few minutes to declutter your bathroom, making it a more pleasant and inviting space. This small act of organization can positively impact your motivation to engage in self-care. A clean and organized space promotes a clean and organized mind.

Visual aids can also be helpful. Create a visual checklist to track your daily hygiene routine. Checking off each task provides a sense of accomplishment and reinforces positive habits. For those who find it challenging to remember to perform hygiene tasks, a simple visual reminder can make a world of difference.

Let's not forget the importance of seeking professional help when needed. If you're struggling to manage your hygiene, don't hesitate to reach out to a therapist or counselor. They can help you identify and address any underlying mental health conditions contributing to the problem. They can provide strategies for managing those conditions and building sustainable self-care practices.

It's vital to remember that self-care isn't selfish; it's essential. It's about acknowledging your worth and taking proactive steps to nurture your physical and emotional well-being. Improving your hygiene is one tangible way to invest in yourself, a small act of self-compassion that can have a surprisingly significant impact on your overall health and happiness. It's a journey, not a race, and every small step forward is a victory worth celebrating. Be patient with yourself, be kind to yourself, and remember that you deserve to feel good, inside and out.

Hygiene and Social Interactions

Now that we've tackled the practical aspects of improving your personal hygiene, let's explore a less obvious, yet equally significant, consequence: the impact on your social interactions. It might seem superficial, but the truth is, how we present ourselves physically profoundly influences how others perceive us and, consequently, how we engage with them. Think of it like this: you wouldn't show up for a job interview in pajamas, right? The same principle applies to our everyday interactions, although the stakes might feel less high.

Good hygiene isn't just about smelling fresh and looking presentable; it's about showing respect for yourself and those around you. It's a silent communication, a nonverbal signal that demonstrates self-care and consideration. When we take care of our physical selves, we're implicitly communicating a sense of self-worth and confidence, which naturally enhances our interactions with others. Conversely, neglecting personal hygiene can create a barrier, inadvertently signaling disinterest or even disregard for social norms.

Imagine this: you're at a social gathering, and you encounter someone with noticeably poor hygiene. Unkempt hair, stained clothing, and body odor can be distracting, making it difficult to focus on the conversation and connect with that person. It's not about judging; it's about acknowledging the human tendency to react to sensory input. These physical cues can subconsciously affect our perception of someone, even if we try to consciously override those first impressions.

This doesn't mean you need to be a model stepping out of a magazine spread. Perfection is unattainable, and striving for it can be incredibly detrimental to mental well-being. We're talking about a reasonable level of cleanliness and presentation, something that demonstrates an effort to care for yourself. That effort, in itself, is what matters most. The impact extends beyond casual encounters. Think about the workplace. While many workplaces understand and are increasingly sensitive to mental health challenges, a consistently unkempt appearance can still unintentionally hinder career progression. It's not always fair, but perceptions, both conscious and unconscious, influence how we're perceived professionally. Maintaining good hygiene can help level the playing field, ensuring that your skills and abilities are judged on their merits, rather than being overshadowed by physical presentation.

This applies equally to romantic relationships. While attraction is multifaceted and goes far beyond hygiene, neglecting basic cleanliness can significantly hinder the development and maintenance of a close relationship. Think about sharing intimate spaces – maintaining a reasonable level of cleanliness is essential for fostering intimacy and reducing potential conflict. This isn't about superficiality; it's about respect and consideration for your partner's comfort and well-being. Again, it's about demonstrating care for yourself and, by extension, for those you share your life with.

Let's look at some specific examples. A simple act like brushing your teeth can have a significant impact. Bad breath, even if unintentional, can create an immediate barrier in social interaction. It can make people reluctant to get close, leading to feelings of isolation and further exacerbating any underlying mental health challenges. On the other hand, fresh breath fosters a sense of confidence and approachability. It's a small, seemingly insignificant detail, yet it speaks volumes.

Similarly, maintaining clean clothing sends a subtle message of respect, both for yourself and for others. While it's fine to express your individuality through fashion choices, unwashed or stained clothes can signal neglect, potentially impacting how people perceive you. Again, it's about striking a balance – expressing your personality without sacrificing basic cleanliness.

Consider the power of a simple handshake. A firm handshake is often associated with confidence and professionalism, but its impact is diminished if your hands are dirty, or your nails are excessively long or unclean. This seemingly small detail can subtly affect the overall impression you make on someone. The details matter, and these seemingly trivial aspects of hygiene build a cumulative impression.

The influence of hygiene extends even to online interactions. While we might not be physically present, the care we take in our appearance in virtual spaces reflects on our self-perception and how we want others to perceive us. A professional headshot for your LinkedIn profile, for instance, projects an image of competence and seriousness, contributing to how you're perceived in the professional world. Similarly, maintaining a well-organized and presentable online presence contributes to how people perceive you.

However, the connection between hygiene and social interactions isn't always straightforward. For individuals battling mental health issues, even basic hygiene routines can feel insurmountable. The debilitating effects of depression, anxiety, or other conditions can make it extraordinarily difficult to manage these simple tasks, leading to a vicious cycle of isolation and low self-esteem. This is precisely where understanding and support are most crucial. Remember that the journey towards better hygiene is not a race; it's a process. Celebrating small victories—a successfully completed shower, freshly washed hair—is paramount. It's about building positive reinforcement, rewarding your efforts and building momentum. Don't focus on perfection, focus on progress.

It's also essential to remember that social interactions are complex and are rarely solely determined by personal hygiene. Personality, communication skills, and emotional intelligence are equally important. But personal hygiene forms a foundational layer; it's the groundwork upon which we build positive social connections. Moreover, there's a crucial connection between self-esteem and hygiene. When we feel good about ourselves, we're more likely to prioritize our physical well-being, including maintaining good hygiene. Conversely, when we neglect our hygiene, we often feel worse about ourselves, leading to a negative feedback loop. Breaking this cycle starts with small, consistent steps, focusing on progress, not perfection. Reward yourself for your efforts and acknowledge your achievements.

Finally, if you're struggling with maintaining good hygiene due to mental health challenges, don't hesitate to seek professional help. A therapist or counselor can provide the support and guidance you need to navigate these difficulties and develop sustainable strategies for self-care. They can help you break down seemingly insurmountable tasks into smaller, manageable steps and develop coping mechanisms for days when the struggle feels overwhelming.

Taking care of your mental health is just as important as taking care of your physical health. They are inextricably linked and addressing both is crucial for overall well-being and successful social interaction.

Remember, asking for help is a sign of strength, not weakness.

You deserve to feel good, both inside and out, and taking care of your hygiene is one step towards achieving that.

Addressing Hygiene Challenges
Addressing hygiene challenges can feel like climbing a mountain when you're already battling mental or physical health issues. The simple act of showering, for instance, can seem insurmountable when depression weighs heavily on your shoulders, or when chronic pain makes even the smallest movements agonizing. It's crucial to understand that these challenges are valid, and they don't reflect a lack of will or self-respect. They're a symptom, not a character flaw.

Let's be honest, the idea of tackling a shower when you're feeling utterly depleted is akin to facing a dragon armed with a water pistol. The energy required feels monumental, and the potential for failure can be incredibly discouraging. This isn't about laziness; it's about the reality of living with a condition that robs you of energy and motivation.

However, there is hope. Overcoming these challenges isn't about suddenly becoming a hygiene superhero overnight. It's about breaking down the seemingly insurmountable task into manageable, bite-sized pieces. Think of it as assembling a Lego castle, one brick at a time. Starting with small, achievable goals is key. Instead of aiming for a full-blown shower, maybe you start with washing your face and hands. Or perhaps just brushing your teeth. Celebrate each small victory, no matter how insignificant it may seem. Positive reinforcement is your secret weapon here.

Reward yourself! Did you manage to brush your teeth? Great! Treat yourself to a cup of tea, a piece of chocolate, or a few minutes of your favorite TV show. These small rewards can make a world of difference in reinforcing positive habits and building momentum. Don't underestimate the power of positive self-talk. Replace negative thoughts like "I can't do this" with "I'm taking one step at a time." Visual aids can be surprisingly helpful. Create a simple checklist, perhaps with pictures instead of words if that's easier. Ticking off each completed task provides a tangible sense of accomplishment and helps track your progress. This visual reminder of your achievements can be incredibly motivating, especially on days when your energy levels are low.

Consider breaking down the task of showering into smaller steps: First, gather your toiletries. Next, turn on the water and adjust the temperature. Then, undress and step into the shower. Each step is a small, achievable goal, minimizing the feeling of being overwhelmed. If you feel too fatigued to finish the entire shower, that's okay. Acknowledge the progress you've made and celebrate that you started.

For those with chronic pain, finding ways to minimize discomfort during hygiene routines is essential. A shower chair can make showering much more manageable, reducing strain on your joints and muscles. Using assistive devices, like long-handled brushes or sponges, can also help you maintain hygiene without exacerbating your pain. Experiment to find what works best for you, remembering that comfort and accessibility are paramount. If you're facing physical limitations that make certain hygiene tasks difficult, such as limited mobility or dexterity, don't hesitate to seek professional assistance. Occupational therapists specialize in helping people adapt their daily routines to accommodate physical limitations. They can assess your individual needs and suggest practical solutions, such as adaptive equipment or modified techniques, making hygiene more accessible and less painful.

Beyond physical limitations, mental health plays a significant role in hygiene challenges. The emotional exhaustion associated with conditions like depression or anxiety can make basic self-care feel impossible. In such cases, self-compassion is crucial. Be kind to yourself. Recognize that you're doing the best you can under difficult circumstances. Avoid self-criticism; it's a counterproductive force that will only make things harder.

Remember that seeking professional help isn't a sign of weakness; it's a sign of strength.

A therapist can provide valuable support and guidance in developing coping mechanisms and strategies for managing the challenges associated with mental health conditions. They can also help you identify and address any underlying issues contributing to your difficulties with hygiene. Cognitive Behavioral Therapy (CBT), for instance, can be highly effective in tackling the negative thought patterns that often accompany mental health struggles and impede self-care.

Consider creating a support system. Talking to trusted friends, family members, or support groups can provide emotional support and encouragement. Sharing your experiences can help alleviate feelings of isolation and shame, reminding you that you're not alone in your struggles. Having someone to check in on you and offer practical assistance can be a lifeline during challenging times.

Building a routine, even a flexible one, can be helpful. Establish a daily or weekly schedule for hygiene tasks, breaking them down into manageable chunks. Consistency, even in small steps, helps to build momentum and create a sense of accomplishment. This routine shouldn't be rigid; flexibility is key, especially when coping with fluctuating energy levels or pain.

It's important to remember that setbacks happen. There will be days when you feel unable to maintain your hygiene routine. Don't let these setbacks derail your progress. Acknowledge them, learn from them, and gently refocus on your goals. Self-compassion is your ally here. Treat yourself with the same understanding and kindness you would offer a friend facing similar challenges.

Maintaining good hygiene is a journey, not a destination. It's a process that involves continuous effort, self-compassion, and a willingness to seek support when needed. It's not about achieving unattainable standards of perfection; it's about making progress, celebrating small victories, and prioritizing your well-being. Remember that you deserve to feel good, both inside and out, and that taking care of your hygiene is an important step towards achieving that sense of well-being and self-respect. Your journey is worthy of celebration; each small step forward is a significant achievement. Keep going. You've got this.

Your therapist won't tell you your hygiene is horrendous, but if others do, she may know how to help.

6. You Are a Victim of Domestic Violence

Your therapist won't call you a victim, but you might be.

It's been suggested that therapists only hear the worst from everyone; that sometimes the scenario didn't *actually* play out as dramatically as a client may describe, or perhaps they may paint a family member in a worse light than is truly accurate. But one thing a client might not always be exaggerating is on issues of their safety. If anything, my experience has been the opposite: a person in the most imminent risk of harm will often downplay their situation so as not to appear "over dramatic" and "exaggerated".

What your therapist may not tell is that she worries about your safety.

Understanding the insidious nature of domestic violence is crucial for escaping its grip. It's not always the dramatic, over the top violent beatings that define abuse; it's often a slow, creeping erosion of self-worth, disguised as "love" or "passion." Domestic violence encompasses a spectrum of controlling behaviors, designed to isolate and subjugate the victim. It's a power imbalance masked in seemingly ordinary interactions. Let's unravel this complex issue and equip you with the tools to recognize it, not just in others, but possibly even within your own life.

First, let me explain what I mean by "domestic violence". It's not simply a heated argument or a momentary loss of temper. Domestic violence is a pattern of coercive and controlling behaviors used to gain power and maintain control over a partner or family member. This pattern can include intimidation, threats, manipulation, physical harm, and sexual assault. Importantly, the violence isn't limited to physical acts; emotional and verbal abuse can be equally damaging and devastating.

Physical abuse, the most readily identifiable form, involves any intentional act causing physical harm. This can range from slapping and shoving to severe beatings, resulting in bruises, broken bones, or even death. However, the physical violence often escalates over time, starting with minor incidents and gradually increasing in severity. The subtle nature of this escalation is precisely why it's so easily missed.

Emotional abuse is far more insidious and often harder to recognize, even for the victim themselves. It aims to erode your self-esteem and sense of self-worth. Think of constant criticism, belittling remarks, and undermining of your accomplishments. It's the insidious drip, drip, drip of negativity that slowly wears you down, making you question your sanity and your ability to function independently. Gaslighting – a form of emotional abuse – involves manipulating you into questioning your own perceptions of reality. Your partner might deny things they've said or done, making you feel confused and doubting yourself. This is a common tactic used to control and isolate the victim.

Verbal abuse is another frequent element, often overlapping with emotional abuse. This involves constant insults, name-calling, threats, and shouting. It's about using words as weapons to control and humiliate. This can be both public and private, further isolating the victim and eroding their confidence. It's not just the words themselves, but the consistent, relentless negativity that wears down the victim's spirit. Think about the cumulative impact of daily verbal assaults – the constant barrage of criticism, the never-ending stream of negativity. It's a form of emotional violence that can be just as damaging as physical violence.

Financial abuse is another insidious form of control. This could involve controlling access to money, preventing you from working, or forcing you to account for every penny you spend. The abuser might take your money, control your bank accounts, or refuse to contribute financially to household expenses. This creates dependency and limits your ability to leave the abusive situation.

It's a subtle way to exert power, leaving the victim financially strapped and dependent on their abuser. Sexual abuse is a severe violation, involving any unwanted sexual act or behavior. This encompasses forced sexual intercourse, unwanted touching, sexual coercion, and threats of sexual violence. It's a violation of bodily autonomy and a form of severe control over the victim. Remember that consent is essential; any sexual act without enthusiastic consent is sexual abuse. Regardless of commitment to one another, a spouse does not have the right to force physical intimacy on their partner without consent.

Digital abuse is a more modern form of control, using technology to monitor and control the victim. This might include tracking their location via GPS, monitoring their social media activity, demanding passwords, or even threatening to share private information. It's a form of control that extends beyond the physical space, creating a sense of constant surveillance and fear.

Isolation is a key tactic used by abusers. They may try to control who you see, where you go, and what you do. They might discourage you from seeing friends and family, limiting your support network and leaving you feeling alone and vulnerable. This isolation makes it harder to seek help and increases the victim's dependence on the abuser.

Controlling behaviors go beyond specific acts of abuse. These are subtle, manipulative tactics designed to gradually chip away at the victim's autonomy. This can involve controlling what you wear, what you eat, or even what you think. They dictate your choices, making you feel like you have no control over your own life. It's a slow, insidious process that leaves the victim feeling helpless and trapped.

Recognizing these signs isn't about finding a checklist and ticking boxes. It's about developing an awareness of patterns and subtle changes in your relationships. If you feel constantly controlled, criticized, or threatened, it's time to take a step back and assess the situation. Does your relationship constantly feel unbalanced, with one person holding more power and control? Are your emotions being manipulated? Are you constantly second-guessing yourself and your perceptions of reality?

Consider these examples: Imagine a partner who constantly criticizes your appearance, making you feel inadequate and insecure. Or perhaps a partner who constantly monitors your whereabouts and accuses you of infidelity, despite no evidence.

These are not isolated incidents; they are part of a pattern of control. Or picture a scenario where a partner threatens to harm themselves or others if you leave the relationship. This is a classic form of coercion designed to keep you trapped. Remember, many victims of domestic violence downplay or minimize the abuse, often believing it's their fault or that they deserve it. This is a common tactic abusers use to maintain control. It's crucial to remember that you are not to blame. Abuse is never the victim's fault.

It's important to look beyond individual incidents and focus on the overall pattern of behavior. A single instance of anger or a harsh word doesn't necessarily signify domestic violence. However, a repeated pattern of controlling behaviors, emotional manipulation, intimidation, and physical violence is a clear indication of a serious problem.

If you or someone you know is experiencing domestic violence, remember that you are not alone. Help is available. Reaching out to a domestic violence hotline, a therapist, or a trusted friend or family member is the first step towards safety and recovery. There are resources and support systems designed to help you break free from this cycle of abuse. Taking that first step is a sign of strength, not weakness.

Don't underestimate the power of recognizing the subtle signs. Early intervention can prevent the escalation of abuse and help victims escape dangerous situations sooner. Remember, your safety and well-being are paramount. You deserve to live a life free from fear and control.

Understanding the Dynamics of Abuse
Understanding the dynamics of abuse requires peeling back the layers of a

relationship built on control, not love. It's about recognizing the subtle ways abusers manipulate and dominate their victims, often leaving lasting emotional scars even after the physical abuse has ended. The core of abusive relationships lies in a significant power imbalance. The abuser actively works to maintain this imbalance, using various tactics to ensure their dominance. This isn't always a brute force approach; it's often a carefully crafted strategy, disguised as concern or even affection.

One of the most crucial elements to grasp is the cyclical nature of abuse. The cycle doesn't always follow a neat, predictable pattern, but it often contains several distinct phases. It typically begins with a period of tension, where minor disagreements escalate into arguments. The tension builds until it culminates in an episode of violence—physical, emotional, or verbal. This violent episode is followed by a period of remorse, where the abuser apologizes profusely, promising it will never happen again. They may shower the victim with gifts, attention, and affection, reinforcing the cycle of hope and manipulation. This "honeymoon" phase is what often traps the victim, making it incredibly difficult to leave. The cycle then repeats, with the tension gradually building again. This pattern makes it incredibly challenging for victims to escape, as they are constantly caught between hope and despair. The abuser expertly plays on these emotions, exploiting the victim's desire for a stable and loving relationship.

The manipulation tactics employed by abusers are diverse and often insidious. Gaslighting, as mentioned previously, is a prime example. The abuser systematically distorts reality, making the victim doubt their own sanity and perceptions. This can range from denying events that have occurred to subtly twisting words and situations to suit their narrative. The victim is left feeling confused and increasingly isolated, believing they are the problem. This manipulation is particularly effective because it erodes the victim's sense of self-worth and their ability to trust their own judgment.

Another common tactic is isolation. Abusers actively work to sever their victim's connections with friends and family. This creates a dependency on the abuser, making it harder for the victim to seek help or escape the abusive situation. The abuser might discourage contact, spread rumors, or even physically prevent the victim from seeing loved ones. This isolation intensifies the victim's feelings of vulnerability and dependence. The abuser becomes the sole source of support, further reinforcing their control.

Financial control is another powerful tool abusers use. They might restrict access to money, prevent the victim from working, or closely monitor their spending. This creates financial dependence and significantly reduces the victim's ability to leave. It's a calculated move to maintain power and control, leaving the victim feeling trapped and powerless. This financial dependence often extends beyond mere control of finances; it can involve controlling access to resources, such as transportation or even basic necessities. In addition to these tactics, abusers often employ intimidation and threats. These threats can range from threats of physical violence to threats of revealing personal information or harming loved ones.

This constant fear keeps the victim submissive and compliant, further reinforcing the abuser's control. The subtle and not-so-subtle threats create a climate of fear that permeates every aspect of the victim's life.

Furthermore, the abusers employ a range of emotional manipulation tactics to maintain control. They might use guilt, shame, or even affection to manipulate the victim's behavior. They often use the victim's empathy and compassion against them. The abuser might feign remorse or vulnerability to garner sympathy and prevent the victim from leaving. They might project their own insecurities and anger onto the victim, blaming them for their own problems.

The impact of these manipulative tactics is devastating. The constant barrage of criticism, control, and intimidation erodes the victim's self-esteem, confidence, and sense of self-worth. Victims often begin to believe the lies and distortions of the abuser, internalizing the blame and accepting responsibility for the abuse. They might isolate themselves further, ashamed and fearing judgment from others. This self-blame and isolation are crucial parts of the abusive cycle, preventing victims from seeking help or leaving the relationship. It is critical to understand that the victim is not responsible for the abuser's actions. Abuse is never the victim's fault. The responsibility for the abuse lies solely with the abuser. This understanding is crucial for both victims and those seeking to help them.

It's essential to differentiate between occasional disagreements and a pattern of abusive behavior. While conflict is a natural part of any relationship, abusive relationships are characterized by a systematic pattern of control and domination. It's not about isolated incidents but rather the consistent repetition of controlling behaviors that creates the abusive dynamic. Recognizing this pattern is critical to breaking free from the cycle.

Many victims struggle to recognize the abuse, often minimizing or rationalizing the abuser's behavior. They may believe they deserve the abuse, or that they can change their abuser. They may fear losing their family, their home, or their financial stability. This fear, coupled with the abuser's manipulative tactics, creates a powerful barrier to escape.

Understanding these dynamics is not simply about identifying specific acts of abuse but understanding the overall context of control and manipulation. It's about recognizing the subtle ways in which power is exerted and maintained within the relationship. It's about recognizing the patterns and cycles of abuse, how these patterns reinforce the abuser's control, and how these patterns create a sense of helplessness in the victim.

Seeking help is a brave step, not a sign of weakness. Reaching out to a domestic violence hotline, a therapist, or a trusted friend or family member is crucial for breaking the cycle and rebuilding a life free from fear and control. There are resources available to help victims regain their independence, their self-esteem, and their sense of safety. Remember, you are not alone. Help is available, and you deserve to live a life free from abuse. Leaving an abusive relationship is not a simple decision; it is often a complex and challenging process. Seeking professional support can greatly aid in navigating this process. This support can include practical help with developing a safety plan, emotional support in processing the trauma of the abuse, and assistance in navigating the legal and logistical aspects of leaving the relationship. The path to healing and recovery is long, but with the right support, it's a journey that is entirely possible.

Creating a Safety Plan

Leaving an abusive relationship is rarely a spontaneous event; it's a carefully planned escape. Thinking you can just "walk out" is like trying to bake a cake without checking the recipe – you might end up with a rather disastrous result. That's where a safety plan comes in. Think of it as your escape recipe, a detailed roadmap guiding you to safety. It's not just about getting out; it's about doing so as safely and effectively as possible.

The first step in crafting your safety plan is identifying safe places. This isn't just about your physical location; it's also about who you can turn to for support. Think about trusted friends or family members who can offer a haven. These could be people who know about the abuse or those who don't but who will offer unconditional support. Prepare them beforehand, even if you don't reveal the full extent of the situation, so they are ready to help. Having a code word or phrase ready can discreetly signal that you need immediate assistance.

Beyond personal contacts, consider safe physical locations. This could be a friend's home, a family member's house, a domestic violence shelter, or even a trusted neighbor's place. Familiarize yourself with the location – the layout, escape routes, and nearby help. Knowing where to go and how to get there quickly can be crucial in an emergency. If you're going to a shelter, research them beforehand. Different shelters cater to specific needs, such as those with children or pets, so ensure you find one that can meet your particular circumstances. Don't hesitate to contact several shelters before making your decision. Remember, feeling safe is paramount.

Next, assemble your essential documents. This is your survival kit, and it should include everything from identification and bank statements to medical records and legal papers. Make copies of everything and store them in a secure location, preferably somewhere outside of your home. A safety deposit box, a friend's house, or even a waterproof, fireproof bag hidden safely outside are all good options. Consider scanning these documents and storing them electronically in a cloud-based system – a password-protected account you can access from anywhere. However, remember physical copies are crucial in many situations.

Financial independence is key. If the abuser controls your finances, start subtly diverting small amounts of money. This may involve opening a secret bank account in your name or using a prepaid debit card. Even small amounts, saved gradually, can make a difference when you need to make a quick escape. If you have a job, explore ways to build up savings discreetly. Look for financial advice resources for people experiencing domestic violence.

Developing an escape strategy is like planning a covert operation. Think about the routes you can take to leave your home quickly and safely. Consider the time of day, when the abuser might be away or less vigilant. Plan alternate routes, in case your primary escape route is blocked. If you have children, practice your escape plan with them, ensuring they know what to do in case of emergency. Create a code word for them to use if they sense danger, enabling them to discreetly alert others.

Your escape route should include a plan for your pets. This is often overlooked, but pets can be the most vulnerable in these situations. Contact your local animal shelter or a pet rescue organization. They often have resources and assistance for victims in your situation. Consider also arranging temporary foster care for your pets with a trusted friend or family member, who knows about your situation, allowing you to leave without worrying about their safety.

Once you've established your escape plan, you'll want to rehearse it. It's like preparing for a big presentation—the more you practice, the smoother the performance goes.

In a crisis, adrenaline can cloud judgment, so it's important to have a well-rehearsed strategy. Practice leaving your home during different times of the day and night to identify potential challenges and develop solutions in advance. This practice reduces the anxiety, and the stress associated with making a quick escape.

Remember, a safety plan is not a one-size-fits-all solution. It's a personalized tool, tailored to your unique circumstances. Your plan must be flexible and adaptable, reflecting the ever-changing dynamics of your situation. Review and update it regularly; it's not a static document but rather a living document reflecting your evolving circumstances and needs. Often, victims of domestic violence underestimate the importance of having a comprehensive support network. We tend to think of support systems as merely emotional support, but they extend far beyond this. Consider a range of support, like legal support, financial advice, emergency housing, and childcare services. Seek out professionals skilled in dealing with domestic violence; they can provide crucial support in navigating the challenging legal processes and provide a much-needed safe space to process emotions.

Furthermore, a safety plan doesn't just encompass the physical act of leaving. It also includes a post-escape plan. Where will you go? How will you secure housing? How will you support yourself financially? Addressing these post-escape logistical issues is as critical as planning your immediate departure. Failure to plan on these issues can significantly impact your success in breaking free from the cycle of abuse.

It's worth noting that some people might initially hesitate to create a safety plan. This hesitation is usually rooted in fear, self-doubt, or a deeply ingrained sense of dependence on the abuser. This hesitancy is perfectly understandable. But remember, creating a safety plan is not an admission of failure; it's an act of empowerment. It's about regaining control, taking proactive steps to protect yourself, and reclaiming your power.

The process itself might feel overwhelming, and that's okay. Take it one step at a time. Begin by identifying one safe place, one trusted person. Collect a few crucial documents. Start small, building momentum as you gain confidence. Remember, even the smallest steps forward are significant progress in this journey. Small victories, such as successfully hiding a small amount of money or practicing a part of the escape route, build resilience and self-belief.

Finally, remember that seeking help is a sign of strength, not weakness. Reaching out to a domestic violence hotline, a therapist, or a trusted friend or family member is a critical step toward breaking free. Don't hesitate to utilize the resources available. There are people who want to help, and you deserve to live a life free from fear and control.

Creating a safety plan is a deeply personal journey. It involves confronting difficult truths, acknowledging vulnerabilities, and making proactive choices to protect yourself. It's a process that demands courage, resilience, and self-compassion. But it's a process that empowers you, granting you the control you deserve in reclaiming your life and building a future free from violence and fear. Remember, you are not alone in this journey. There are people and resources dedicated to helping you achieve safety, reclaim your life and heal. The road ahead may be challenging, but with careful planning and the right support, you can and will escape this cycle, stepping into a life of freedom, peace, and self-respect.

Seeking Help and Support

Now that you have meticulously crafted your safety plan – your personal escape recipe, if you will – let's talk about the unsung hero of this whole endeavor: seeking help. Think of it as adding the secret ingredient that elevates your escape from a hurried dash to a strategic maneuver. Because let's face it, escaping domestic violence is rarely a solo mission; it's a team effort, and you deserve the best support team possible. Many folks believe that reaching out for help is a sign of weakness. This is an old stigma that is unfortunately alive and well today.

Asking for help is a testament to your strength, your resilience, and your unwavering commitment to building a better life for yourself. It's the equivalent of admitting you need a helping hand when carrying a ridiculously oversized suitcase – it doesn't diminish your strength; it just makes the journey smarter and less exhausting.

So, where do you find this invaluable support? Let's explore some key resources, starting with the often overlooked but incredibly important: domestic violence shelters. These aren't just places to crash for a night; they are lifelines. They offer a haven, temporary housing, counseling, legal assistance, and often connections to other support services. Think of them as your all-inclusive resort for escaping the cycle of abuse – but without the pesky vacation price tag.

Finding the right shelter is crucial. Some shelters specialize in working with women, others cater to families with children, and some even welcome pets. Don't be afraid to call multiple shelters to find the perfect fit for you and your unique circumstances. Research them beforehand, checking for things like their policies, the services they offer, and the general vibe (you want a place that feels safe and supportive, not like another source of stress). Think of it as house-hunting for your temporary sanctuary. You deserve a place where you feel comfortable and secure. Beyond shelters, support groups provide a space for sharing experiences, connecting with others who understand your situation, and gaining invaluable emotional support. These groups offer a powerful sense of community, helping you realize you're not alone in this journey. Sharing your story, hearing others' stories, and knowing there are people who genuinely "get it" is incredibly validating and empowering. It's like joining a secret society of superheroes – you're not just fighting your battle; you're fighting alongside a team that knows the terrain. Many shelters and community centers offer these groups, and some are even available online.

Now, let's talk about something that often gets a bad rap – law enforcement. While the system isn't perfect, it's a valuable tool you shouldn't hesitate to utilize. If you are in immediate danger, call emergency services. Do not hesitate. Your safety is paramount. Reporting the abuse can trigger a legal process that can lead to protection orders, restraining orders, and even criminal charges against the abuser. Again, this isn't about blaming you; it's about ensuring your safety and potentially protecting others from similar experiences. Legal aid organizations can be invaluable allies in navigating the complicated legal system. They can assist with protective orders, divorce proceedings, custody battles, and other legal matters. They can help you make sense of complex legal jargon, guide you through the process, and provide the legal support you need to secure your future. Consider them your legal Sherpas, guiding you safely through the treacherous mountains of the legal world.

Financial assistance is often overlooked but incredibly crucial. Escaping domestic violence can leave you vulnerable financially. Many organizations offer financial aid programs, job training resources, and support for securing stable employment. There are funds available to help you cover housing costs, food, transportation, and other essential needs as you rebuild your life. These resources are like emergency financial airbags – helping you land softly after a tough financial crash. Childcare and other support services are essential if you have children. Shelters often provide childcare services, enabling you to access support and resources while knowing your children are in a safe and caring environment. There are also many other childcare assistance programs that you can access. Your kids deserve a haven too and finding support to help you ensure that is vital.

Remember, reaching out for help doesn't mean you've failed; it means you're actively taking control of your life and choosing safety. There is no shame in seeking support. In fact, it's the bravest, smartest thing you can do.

Here is a list of resources you can utilize, keeping in mind that access and availability may vary by location:

The National Domestic Violence Hotline: This hotline offers 24/7 support and resources for victims of domestic violence. *1.800.799.7233* or *text BEGIN to 88788*

Local Domestic Violence Shelters: A quick online search for "domestic violence shelters near me" will bring up relevant options in your area.

Legal Aid Organizations: These organizations provide legal assistance to individuals who cannot afford legal representation. Your local bar association can be a good starting point for finding these services. *Varies by state.*

Mental Health Professionals: Therapists and counselors specializing in trauma can provide essential support during this challenging time. Finding the right professional support isn't always straightforward.

You will want to work with someone who understands the nuances of domestic violence, who can validate your experiences, and who can help you develop healthy coping mechanisms. It might take some searching, some trial and error, to find the right fit. That's okay. Keep looking until you find a therapist who makes you feel heard, respected, and empowered. Think of it as finding the perfect pair of shoes – you'll know when you've found the perfect fit.

Remember, there is no quick fix for escaping domestic violence. It's a process, a journey, with its ups and downs, its moments of triumph and moments of doubt. But every step you take, every resource you utilize, every person you trust, brings you closer to the life of safety, freedom, and self-respect you deserve. You are not alone in this fight. Reach out. Connect. Build your support network. Your strength is not measured by how long you endure the abuse, but by the courage you show in escaping it and rebuilding your life. And remember, seeking help isn't a sign of weakness; it's a testament to your resilience, your strength, and your unwavering commitment to a brighter future. You deserve that future, and you have the power to create it. Trust in yourself, trust in your strength, and trust in the support that's available to you. You've got this.

Recovery and Healing from Abuse
The escape is just the first step on a long and winding road. Leaving an abusive relationship doesn't magically erase the trauma; it simply opens the door to healing. The emotional toll of domestic violence is immense, often leaving survivors grappling with a complex tapestry of feelings: fear, anger, guilt, shame, confusion, and a profound sense of loss. It's like waking up from a long, disturbing dream, only to find that the lingering effects are very real. You might feel adrift, unsure of who you are outside the context of the abusive relationship. This is completely normal. It's the aftershock of a powerful earthquake that has shaken your very foundations.

One of the most common struggles is grappling with feelings of guilt and shame. Abusers often manipulate their victims into believing they are somehow to blame for the abuse. They might whisper insidious doubts, twisting events to make their victims feel responsible for the abuser's actions. This insidious gaslighting can leave deep scars, making it incredibly difficult for survivors to recognize that they are not at fault.

Remember this: abuse is never the victim's fault. Never. Period. Understanding this is the first crucial step towards reclaiming your self-worth. Healing from this emotional damage is not a sprint; it's a marathon. It requires patience, self-compassion, and consistent effort. There's no magic pill, no overnight fix. It's about gently, lovingly piecing your life back together, one shard at a time. And the process might be messy, unpredictable, and occasionally painful. But remember, that's okay. Allow yourself to feel the full spectrum of your emotions without judgment. Don't try to bottle them up; instead, acknowledge them, process them, and let them gradually dissipate.

Think of your emotional healing as tending to a wounded garden.

You wouldn't expect a flower to bloom overnight after being ravaged by a storm. It takes time, nurturing, and consistent care.

Similarly, your emotional recovery requires tender attention. That might involve setting aside time for self-care, engaging in activities you enjoy, practicing mindfulness, or seeking professional support.

Don't be afraid to ask for help; you are not alone in this.

Seeking professional help from a therapist or counselor specializing in trauma is crucial. These professionals possess the skills and expertise to guide you through the complex process of healing. They can provide a safe and supportive space for you to explore your emotions, unpack the trauma, and develop healthy coping mechanisms. They can also help you identify and challenge the negative thought patterns that might be holding you back from moving forward. Remember the shoe analogy from earlier? Finding the right therapist might require some trial and error, but it's an investment in yourself and your future well-being that is invaluable.

Building a strong support network is another vital component of recovery. Connect with friends, family members, or support groups who understand what you're going through. Sharing your experiences can be incredibly cathartic and validating. It can help you realize you're not alone, that others have navigated similar challenges, and that healing is possible. These connections provide a lifeline, a sense of belonging, and the reassurance that you're not invisible in the face of unimaginable pain.

Rebuilding your life after escaping abuse is about more than just emotional healing; it's also about creating a new narrative, a new reality. This involves setting boundaries, prioritizing your needs, and focusing on self-discovery. It's about re-learning what healthy relationships look like, building self-esteem, and reclaiming your sense of self. This isn't a simple task, it's a significant undertaking that requires courage, perseverance, and self-belief.

Consider the example of Jennifer, a woman who escaped a decade-long abusive marriage. Leaving felt impossible initially; the fear and intimidation were overwhelming. But with the help of a domestic violence shelter and a supportive therapist, she found the strength to leave.

Her recovery was gradual, filled with setbacks and moments of self-doubt. There were days when the past threatened to engulf her, but with the unwavering support of her therapist and her new support network of friends, she began slowly building a new life for herself and her children. She enrolled in college, pursued her lifelong dream of becoming a teacher, and gradually rebuilt her shattered sense of self-esteem. Her journey wasn't easy, but it was a testament to her remarkable resilience and unwavering determination.

Another client, Daniel, was abused by his partner for several years. He carried the shame and silence for far too long before seeking help, partly due to societal expectations and ingrained gender roles. Eventually, his friend convinced him to attend a support group for male survivors of domestic abuse. The support group allowed him to share his story without judgment, to connect with others who understood, and to find the strength to begin healing. Through therapy, he addressed the underlying emotional wounds that contributed to his vulnerability in the relationship, and he eventually found a healthy and supportive relationship where his voice was heard and valued. These are just two examples, and every journey is unique. Healing isn't linear; it's a winding path filled with ups and downs, moments of progress and moments of regression. It's essential to be patient with yourself, to celebrate your small victories, and to acknowledge that setbacks are part of the process. Allow yourself to grieve the loss of what was, while simultaneously embracing the promise of what could be. Embrace the opportunity to create a future where you are safe, secure, and empowered.

Rebuilding your life after escaping abuse is a profound act of self-love and self-respect. It's about reclaiming your power, choosing your own path, and creating a future where you flourish. It requires courage, perseverance, and unwavering belief in your ability to heal and thrive. Remember, you are not alone in this journey. There is a vast network of support waiting to help you, to empower you, and to guide you toward a brighter future. And amidst the darkness, remember to look for the glimmers of hope, the small victories, the gradual progress. They are there, often hidden within the cracks, patiently waiting to be discovered. Focus on those glimmers, nurture them, and let them illuminate your path towards healing and a life of freedom and happiness. It's about reclaiming your narrative, rewriting your story, and ensuring that the next chapter is filled with strength, hope, and the unwavering commitment to a life you deserve. You are strong. You are resilient. And you are not alone. The path to healing may be long, but the destination – a life free from abuse – is worth the journey. You've already taken the biggest step – leaving the abusive situation. Remember that you are capable of amazing things. Remember to be kind to yourself throughout this process; you deserve all the compassion and understanding you give to others. You are worthy of love, happiness, and a life free from violence.

Your therapist won't tell you you're not safe at home because you already know this.

7. Quit Your Job

Your therapist is not going to tell you to quit your job. But perhaps you need to.

Leaving a job, even a toxic one, often feels like leaping from a cliff into the unknown. The familiar, even if unpleasant, is replaced by a terrifying void of uncertainty. This fear, this anxiety about the unknown, is a potent force, often overshadowing the relief and excitement that should accompany escaping a difficult work environment. It's a completely understandable response, and it's something we all grapple with at various points in our lives, not just when leaving a job.

Think about it – how many times have you avoided something, not because it was inherently bad, but because you didn't know what to expect?

The fear of the unknown is primal. Our brains are wired to prefer the predictable, the known - over the unpredictable, the unknown.

This is a survival mechanism humans have honed in on over the ages; avoiding the unknown kept our ancestors safe from predators and other dangers. While today's dangers are different – they're more likely to involve a missed mortgage payment than a saber-toothed tiger – our brains still react in the same way. That sudden lurch in your stomach, that knot of tension in your chest? That's your animal brain, screaming, *"Danger! Unknown territory!"*

One of the most significant anxieties associated with leaving a job is the fear of unemployment. This is especially true in today's economic climate, where job security is often a myth, and even stable companies can undergo sudden downsizing. The thought of losing your income, the potential for financial instability – the pressure to support yourself and your family – it's enough to keep anyone tethered to a job they hate. The fear isn't just about losing your paycheck; it's about losing your identity, your sense of purpose, your very sense of self-worth. For many, their job is more than just a source of income; it's a significant part of their social identity.

Let's consider the example of Mark, a software engineer who had toiled for ten years at a company that had slowly become increasingly toxic. The constant pressure, the unrealistic deadlines, the undermining from a particularly nasty manager – it was slowly chipping away at his mental health. He yearned to leave, to find a company where his skills and creativity were valued. But the fear of unemployment, of the financial implications, kept him chained to his desk, despite the growing turmoil inside. He worried about the potential job search, the interviews, the uncertainty of whether he could find another position that paid as well. The fear of the unknown kept him paralyzed.

Mark's story isn't unique. Many people, particularly those with families or significant financial responsibilities, feel a tremendous pressure to stay in unfulfilling jobs out of sheer financial necessity. They might delay their own happiness, their own well-being, out of a fear of the financial repercussions of leaving. It's a difficult tightrope to walk, and it often involves weighing the immediate discomfort of the current situation against the potentially greater discomfort of the unknown future.

Beyond the fear of unemployment lies the fear of financial insecurity. Even if you have a job lined up, the transition period between jobs can be financially stressful. There might be a gap in pay, potential delays in receiving benefits, or unexpected expenses that arise during the transition. This fear is particularly acute for those who live paycheck to paycheck, who don't have a significant savings cushion to fall back on. The worry about making rent, paying bills, putting food on the table – these very real concerns often override the desire for a better work environment.

Consider the example of Sarah, a single mother who worked as a waitress. She was chronically overworked, underpaid, and subjected to verbal abuse from some customers. She desperately wanted to leave, but she knew that finding another job that provided the same level of income and benefits would be a huge challenge. The fear of not being able to provide for her child, of falling into poverty, kept her stuck in a job that was slowly destroying her. She knew that staying was detrimental to her mental health, yet the fear of financial instability was a powerful deterrent to change.

Then there's the broader fear of uncertainty about the future. Leaving a job, regardless of the circumstances, involves a significant leap into the unknown. You're stepping away from a familiar routine, from an established structure, into a space where the path ahead is unclear. The lack of control, the absence of a predefined plan, can be incredibly anxiety-inducing for many people. This uncertainty extends beyond the financial aspect; it encompasses all aspects of your life.

This lack of control over the future can manifest in various ways. It might be the fear of never finding a better job, or the fear of never achieving your career goals. It might be the fear of not being able to replicate the social connections and relationships you've built at your current job. It might even be the fear of simply not knowing what the next chapter of your life will look like. The feeling of having no roadmap, no predetermined route, can be disorienting and unnerving for many.

Think of Stephanie, a project manager who left her job after feeling chronically undervalued and underappreciated. She had a new job lined up, but the uncertainty about the team dynamics, the corporate culture, and the long-term prospects of the new company left her feeling anxious. The fear wasn't about financial instability; it was about the unknown aspects of the new work environment and the potential for repeating past negative experiences. This anxiety, the fear of the unknown variables, is a significant aspect of many people's hesitancy to leave a job.

So how do we navigate these fears? How do we move from anxiety to action? The first step is acknowledging the fears. Don't try to suppress or ignore them. Recognize that they're valid, that they're a normal response to a significant life change. Give yourself permission to feel anxious, to feel uncertain. This acceptance is crucial.

Once you've acknowledged your fears, it's time to start breaking them down into smaller, more manageable pieces. Instead of focusing on the overwhelming uncertainty of the future, focus on the immediate next steps. Create a plan, a roadmap, even if it's a rudimentary one. This can involve things like updating your resume, networking with people in your industry, researching potential job opportunities. Each small step forward, however insignificant it may seem, reduces the feeling of being overwhelmed by the unknown.

Financial planning is essential. Before leaving your job, take stock of your finances. Assess your savings, your expenses, and develop a budget for the transition period. If possible, start building an emergency fund. This will alleviate some of the financial stress and give you more confidence to take the leap. Additionally, it's crucial to build a strong support network. Talk to friends, family members, mentors, or career counselors. Sharing your anxieties can help to reduce their power. Often, simply verbalizing your fears can help to diffuse them. Remember, you're not alone in feeling this way. Many people experience similar anxieties when leaving a job.

Consider seeking professional help. A therapist or counselor can provide tools and strategies to manage your anxiety and develop healthy coping mechanisms. They can help you challenge negative thought patterns, build your confidence, and develop a plan for managing the transition.

Finally, remember that the unknown isn't necessarily bad. It's full of potential, of opportunity, of new possibilities. Leaving a job, even a comfortable one, opens up a new path, full of new experiences and new growth. Embrace the unknown, take risks, and trust in your ability to adapt and overcome. The fear of the unknown will always be present to some extent, but with careful planning, support, and self-compassion, it can be effectively managed, allowing you to move forward into a brighter future. And who knows, what you find on the other side might just surprise you in the most wonderful way.

Building Confidence for a Job Search

Building confidence in yourself during a job search after leaving a challenging role isn't about magically erasing anxiety; it's about equipping yourself with tools and strategies to navigate it effectively. Think of it like this: you wouldn't jump into a freezing lake without first warming up; similarly, diving headfirst into a job search without preparation is a recipe for increased anxiety. We've explored the depths of the fear of the unknown, the financial anxieties, and the uncertainty that accompanies such a major life transition. Now, let's equip ourselves to face those fears head-on.

The first step in building confidence is often the most daunting: updating your resume and cover letter. For many, this feels like staring into the abyss of self-doubt. "Am I good enough? Will my skills even be relevant?" These questions are common, especially when you've been in a job that didn't fully utilize your potential or, worse, actively undermined your self-worth. But here's the thing: your resume isn't a reflection of your past failures; it's a marketing document showcasing your accomplishments and potential.

Treat your resume like a finely crafted cocktail – it needs the right mix of ingredients to be truly effective. Start by identifying your key skills and accomplishments. Don't just list your responsibilities; quantify your achievements. Instead of saying "Managed social media accounts," try "Increased social media engagement by 30% in six months through targeted content creation and strategic campaign development." See the difference? The second statement is far more powerful, demonstrating tangible results and showcasing your capabilities.

Your cover letter is where you get to personalize your marketing pitch. Think of it as your elevator pitch, a chance to highlight your unique skills and experiences that make you a perfect fit for the specific role and company. Research the company thoroughly before writing your cover letter; show them you're genuinely interested, not just sending out generic applications. Find a common thread between your skills and their needs and weave a compelling narrative that demonstrates your understanding of their business and how you can contribute to their success.

Let's face it: interviewing can feel like a high-stakes game of verbal gymnastics. The pressure to impress, to sell yourself, can be overwhelming. However, the key to successful interviewing isn't memorizing canned responses; it's about practicing honest and authentic communication. Prepare for common interview questions but also anticipate some curveballs. Practice answering questions aloud, ideally with a friend or mentor who can offer feedback.

Record yourself and review your performance; it might feel awkward, but it's invaluable in identifying areas for improvement. One often overlooked aspect of confidence building is practicing your storytelling skills. Think about your previous experiences –both successes and failures – as valuable learning opportunities. Instead of focusing solely on the positive, learn to articulate how you've learned and grown from challenges. This shows maturity, resilience, and a willingness to learn, qualities that employers highly value.

Networking, (often a dreaded word for introverts), is a crucial element of a successful job search. It's not about schmoozing or being fake; it's about building genuine connections. Start by reaching out to your existing professional network – former colleagues, classmates, professors. Inform them of your job search and seek their advice and support. Attend industry events, online forums, and workshops to expand your network and learn about new opportunities.

Consider informational interviews. These are informal conversations with people in your field, where you ask questions about their career path, their insights into the industry, and their advice for someone looking to enter or advance in that field. It's a low-pressure way to expand your knowledge, build connections, and learn about unadvertised job openings. Remember, people are generally happy to help others, especially if approached genuinely and respectfully.

Beyond these practical strategies, consider your self-talk. The internal narrative you create about yourself significantly impacts your confidence. Challenge negative self-talk ("I'm not good enough," "I'll never find a job") by replacing it with positive affirmations ("I have valuable skills," "I'm capable of finding a fulfilling role"). Keep a journal to track your progress, celebrate your achievements (even small ones), and identify areas where you can further improve your job search strategy.

Visualize your success. Imagine yourself acing interviews, receiving job offers, and thriving in your new role. Visualization is a powerful tool that can rewire your brain to focus on positive outcomes, reducing anxiety and boosting your confidence. This isn't about wishful thinking; it's about programming your mind for success. One technique to counter job search anxiety is to establish a consistent daily routine. This includes setting realistic goals for each day (e.g., updating your LinkedIn profile, sending out five applications, networking with one contact). The sense of accomplishment from achieving daily goals helps counter feelings of helplessness and builds momentum in your job search.

Remember the examples from earlier chapters: Mark, Sarah, and Lisa. They all faced significant anxieties, but their journeys didn't end there. Mark, through meticulous resume updates and thoughtful networking, secured a role at a company that valued his skills. Sarah, with the support of friends and family, found a job with better pay and working conditions. Lisa, by carefully researching potential employers and preparing extensively for interviews, successfully transitioned to a more fulfilling role. Their stories highlight that overcoming job search anxiety is achievable with dedication, planning, and self-belief.

Finally, remember to *prioritize self-care*. A job search can be incredibly stressful, so it's crucial to take breaks, engage in activities you enjoy, and maintain a healthy lifestyle. Exercise, healthy eating, sufficient sleep, and mindfulness practices can significantly reduce stress levels and enhance your overall well-being. Think of this as investing in your own resilience, equipping yourself to handle the challenges of the job search and emerge stronger and more confident on the other side. The job search is a marathon, not a sprint, and building confidence is a gradual process. Be kind to yourself, celebrate your successes, and remember you're not alone in this journey.

Managing Financial Concerns
The emotional rollercoaster of job loss often overshadows the very real financial anxieties that follow. While the emotional aspects are crucial to address, neglecting the practicalities of managing your finances can exacerbate stress and prolong the job search process.

Let's shift our focus to the nuts and bolts of navigating this challenging financial terrain. Think of this as creating a financial safety net – a crucial part of your overall job search strategy. The first step, and often the most daunting, is facing your finances head-on. This doesn't require an MBA; it simply requires honesty and a willingness to understand your current financial landscape.

Pull out your bank statements, credit card bills, and any other relevant financial documents. Don't shy away from the numbers; they are simply data points, not reflections of your worth. Now, let's build a budget. I know, I know, "budget" sounds incredibly boring, about as exciting as watching paint dry. But hear me out: a budget is your financial roadmap. It helps you visualize where your money is going and allows you to identify areas where you can cut back. There are countless budgeting apps and spreadsheets available, but the core principles remain the same: track your income and expenses, categorize them (housing, food, transportation, etc.), and identify areas where you can adjust.

Remember, budgeting isn't about deprivation; it's about making conscious choices about how you spend your money. Small changes can make a significant difference. For example, switching to a cheaper phone plan, reducing your streaming services, or packing your lunch instead of eating out can free up considerable funds over time. Think of it as a financial detox – cleansing your spending habits to create space for smarter financial decisions.

Let's be realistic: cutting back isn't always enough. If you're facing immediate financial challenges, exploring savings options is critical. Do you have any emergency savings? This is where the importance of having a financial cushion before a job change becomes abundantly clear. Even a small emergency fund can provide a sense of security during this uncertain period. If your savings are depleted, don't despair. There are options. Consider contacting your bank or credit union to see if they offer any financial assistance programs or hardship options. Many institutions have programs designed to help customers facing temporary financial difficulties. These programs might include temporary interest rate reductions, payment deferrals, or even small loans with favorable terms. Don't hesitate to reach out; they're there to help their customers navigate tough times.

Another potential source of financial assistance is government programs. Depending on your location and circumstances, you may be eligible for unemployment benefits, food stamps, or other forms of social support. Navigating these programs can be complex, but numerous resources are available to help you understand the eligibility criteria and application process. Don't be afraid to seek assistance from local charities, non-profit organizations, or government agencies. They're often a wealth of information and support.

Beyond government programs, consider exploring options like selling unused items, freelancing, or taking on temporary work. Selling items, you no longer need can provide a quick influx of cash, while freelancing offers a flexible way to earn income while you're actively searching for a new job. Temporary work, even if it's not directly related to your field, can provide a much-needed financial buffer. The key is to be resourceful and explore all available options.

Now, let's talk about debt. If you have outstanding debts, such as credit card balances or loans, reaching out to your creditors is crucial. Explain your situation and explore options for debt management, such as payment plans or temporary interest rate reductions. Many creditors are willing to work with customers who are experiencing financial hardship. Proactive communication can help you avoid late payments and the negative impact on your credit score.

It's important to remember that seeking financial help doesn't equate to failure. It demonstrates resourcefulness and a proactive approach to managing a challenging situation. Many people find themselves in similar circumstances, and accessing available resources is a sign of strength, not weakness.

Let's look at some examples. Imagine Sarah, a single mother who recently lost her job. Facing mounting bills and the prospect of feeding her children, she immediately created a detailed budget, eliminating non-essential expenses. She also contacted her bank to explore options for a temporary loan and applied for unemployment benefits. Her proactive approach, coupled with the support of friends and family, helped her navigate this difficult period.

Consider Ben, a freelance graphic designer who experienced a sudden lull in projects. He leveraged his savings and began taking on smaller, temporary projects to maintain a steady income stream. He also reached out to his professional network, letting them know he was available for freelance work. His network proved invaluable, leading to several new projects and providing him with a financial lifeline.

Finally, consider Lisa, a marketing professional who had built up a significant emergency fund. Although losing her job was a setback, her savings allowed her to focus on her job search without the added pressure of immediate financial worries. This allowed her to dedicate her energy to finding a role that truly aligned with her skills and aspirations. This is a testament to the power of financial preparation and planning.

These examples highlight the diverse approaches people take when dealing with job loss. There's no one-size-fits-all solution. The key is to be proactive, resourceful, and to seek help when needed. Remember, navigating financial anxieties during a job search is a marathon, not a sprint. Take it one step at a time, celebrate small victories, and remember that you are not alone in this journey. With careful planning and proactive action, you can successfully manage your financial concerns and emerge stronger on the other side. This financial stability will, in turn, bolster your confidence and enhance your job search efforts. It's about building a solid foundation, not just finding a job; it's about building a resilient you.

Exploring New Career Opportunities

Now that we've established a solid financial foundation, let's turn our attention to the exciting, albeit sometimes daunting, prospect of exploring new career opportunities. Losing a job can feel like a door slamming shut, but it's also an open window to a world of possibilities. Think of it as a career reset, a chance to reassess your skills, passions, and long-term goals.

The first step in this exciting adventure is self-discovery. What are you truly good at? What energizes you? What tasks make you lose track of time because you're so engrossed? Don't just think about your past job titles; delve deeper into your accomplishments. What projects did you excel at? What feedback did you consistently receive? These are clues to your strengths and hidden talents.

Consider making a list, a mind map, or even a collage – whatever creative method best suits your style. Write down every skill you possess, from the obvious (like proficiency in a specific software) to the less apparent (like exceptional communication skills or the ability to motivate teams). Don't underestimate the power of "soft skills"—things like problem-solving, critical thinking, adaptability, and teamwork. These are highly valued across a wide range of industries. If you're feeling stuck, ask friends, family, or former colleagues for their perspective. Their insights might surprise you.

Once you have a clearer picture of your skillset, it's time to research potential job opportunities. The internet is your oyster! Job boards like Indeed, LinkedIn, Monster, and Glassdoor are excellent starting points. But don't limit yourself to online searches. Network! Reach out to your professional contacts, attend industry events (even virtual ones), and inform your network of your job search. You never know what opportunity might arise from a casual conversation.

When researching potential jobs, consider factors beyond just the salary. Think about the company culture, the work-life balance, opportunities for growth, and the overall work environment. Does the company's mission resonate with your values? Does the work sound engaging and challenging? These are crucial factors to consider, as finding a job you enjoy is just as important as securing a paycheck.

Let's look at some examples to illustrate this point. Suppose you're a highly organized and detail-oriented individual with excellent communication skills and experience in project management. These skills are transferable to a wide array of jobs, from administrative roles to marketing coordination, event planning, or even operations management. Your research might lead you to explore positions in these fields, comparing job descriptions, company cultures, and salary expectations.

Or consider someone with a background in customer service. Excellent interpersonal skills and problem-solving abilities aren't limited to retail or call center jobs. These skills translate well to roles in sales, human resources, teaching, or even social work. A deep dive into job postings in these areas will reveal a broader range of opportunities than initially perceived. For those with technical skills, such as programming or data analysis, the options are vast and ever evolving. The tech industry is constantly seeking skilled professionals, and exploring different sectors within tech— from software development to cybersecurity to data science—can unveil many exciting career paths. Similarly, someone with strong writing and communication skills might find themselves exploring opportunities in journalism, marketing, technical writing, or content creation.

The key here is to be open-minded and explore options that might not immediately seem related to your previous experience. Sometimes, a slight career shift can lead to unexpected fulfillment and professional growth. Remember, you're not limited to what you've done before; you're empowered by what you *can* do.

Once you've identified several potential career paths, it's time to develop a plan. This doesn't need to be a rigid, inflexible document; rather, it should be a flexible roadmap to guide your job search. It should include your target job titles, a list of companies you're interested in, a timeline for applying to positions, and strategies for networking. Regularly review and update this plan as you learn more about different opportunities and refine your goals.

This plan should also incorporate strategies for showcasing your skills and experience. Update your resume and LinkedIn profile to highlight your transferable skills and accomplishments. Prepare compelling cover letters that demonstrate your enthusiasm and qualifications for each specific position. Practice your interviewing skills— roleplaying with a friend or utilizing online resources can significantly boost your confidence. And remember, the job search itself is a skill that develops with practice and persistence.

Let's consider a few case studies: Imagine Alex, a former accountant who discovered a passion for data visualization during their previous role. By honing their technical skills and networking within the data analytics field, Alex successfully transitioned into a data analyst position, leveraging their existing accounting background for a more fulfilling career. Or consider Sarah, a marketing manager who felt burnt out by the corporate world. She identified a desire for more flexibility and work-life balance and leveraged her writing and communication skills to successfully launch her own freelance content creation business. This allowed her to pursue her passion while establishing her own schedule.

Then there's Mark, an experienced software engineer who realized he was more passionate about teaching than coding. He used his technical expertise to develop online courses and landed a part-time position teaching programming at a local community college, combining his love of technology with his newfound passion for education.

These examples highlight the transformative power of actively exploring new career opportunities. It's a journey of self-discovery and strategic planning. It requires honest self-assessment, thorough research, and a proactive approach to networking. Don't be afraid to step outside your comfort zone and explore paths you might not have considered before. Remember, the anxiety of leaving a job often stems from uncertainty. By proactively exploring new opportunities and creating a well-defined plan, you can transform that uncertainty into excitement and anticipation for the next chapter of your career. The journey may have its bumps, but the destination – a career that aligns with your skills and passions – is well worth the effort.

You've already demonstrated resilience by navigating the emotional and financial challenges of job loss; now, embrace this opportunity to build a career that truly fulfills you. And remember, even if your initial attempts don't immediately lead to your dream job, every step forward is progress, every application submitted, every interview attended brings you closer to the right fit. Persistence, combined with a proactive and resourceful approach, is the key to unlocking your ideal career path.

Building a Support Network

Now, let's talk about something equally crucial to navigating this career transition: your support network. You've taken the brave first steps towards a new chapter, but remember, you don't have to walk this path alone. Building a strong support system is as vital as updating your resume or researching job postings. It's about surrounding yourself with people who can offer encouragement, practical advice, and a listening ear when the self-doubt creeps in.

Think of your support network as your personal cheering squad, your wise counsel, and your reality check all rolled into one. They're the people who will celebrate your small victories – like landing an interview or mastering a new skill – and help you navigate the inevitable setbacks. Let's start with the closest members of your circle: family and friends. These are the folks who know you best, have seen you at your highs and lows, and can offer unconditional support, even if they don't understand the intricacies of your professional life. Their role isn't necessarily to give career advice (unless they're experts in your field!), but rather to provide emotional sustenance. A listening ear, a shoulder to cry on, or a comforting distraction can make a world of difference when you're feeling overwhelmed.

Remember that time you spilled coffee all over your presentation five minutes before a big meeting? Or that time your computer crashed just as you were about to submit a critical report? We all have those moments where professional life throws us a curveball. Your family and friends are there to remind you that you're human, that mistakes happen, and that you're capable of bouncing back. Their empathy and unwavering belief in you can be incredibly powerful, providing a much-needed boost to your confidence and resilience.

Beyond your immediate family and friends, consider expanding your network to include people who share your professional aspirations or have experience navigating similar transitions. Think of joining professional organizations, attending industry events (even virtual ones are great!), or connecting with mentors or career coaches. These individuals can offer valuable insights, share their experiences, and provide practical advice based on their own journeys.

For example, if you're transitioning into a completely new field, a mentor in that field could be invaluable. They can offer guidance on the necessary skills and certifications, introduce you to key contacts, and help you navigate the unspoken rules of the new industry. They've walked the path before, and their wisdom can save you time, energy, and frustration.

Don't underestimate the power of online communities as well. Numerous online forums and groups are dedicated to career transitions, specific industries, or even particular job searches. These platforms provide opportunities to connect with others facing similar challenges, exchange advice, share resources, and even find potential collaborators or job leads. It's a powerful way to combat feelings of isolation and build a sense of camaraderie during a potentially isolating experience.

And then there's the often overlooked, yet tremendously helpful resource: career counselors. These professionals are trained to help individuals navigate career transitions, identify their strengths and weaknesses, develop effective job search strategies, and improve their interviewing skills. They can provide objective feedback on your resume and cover letter, help you define your career goals, and offer guidance on salary negotiations. Think of a career counselor as your personal career GPS. They can help you plot a course towards your desired destination, even when the road ahead seems unclear or confusing. They can help you identify blind spots in your job search strategy, offer insights into your transferable skills, and boost your confidence during the sometimes-daunting process of interviewing. Many career services are available through universities, community colleges, and even employment agencies. Some offer free services, while others charge a fee. Research your options to find a counselor who best fits your needs and budget. Remember, the investment in your career future can be invaluable.

Building a support network is an ongoing process, not a one-time event. It requires nurturing and maintenance. Make time to connect with your support system regularly, share your experiences (both good and bad), and reciprocate their support by being there for them as well. The relationships you forge during this transition can last a lifetime. A strong support network will not only help you navigate your career transition but will also enrich your life beyond your professional pursuits.

Remember that seeking help is a sign of strength, not weakness. Acknowledging that you need support is a crucial first step towards building resilience and achieving your career goals. Don't be afraid to ask for help, whether it's from family, friends, professional contacts, or career counselors. The support you receive will not only ease the emotional burden but will also enhance your chances of success.

The journey of leaving a job and finding a new one is often a complex emotional rollercoaster. There will be moments of excitement, uncertainty, frustration, and even self-doubt. But throughout it all, remember the power of your support network. These are the people who will lift you up when you're down, provide guidance when you're lost, and celebrate your successes with you. Lean on them, nurture these relationships, and allow them to be your anchor during this transformative period in your career. And in turn, be there for others in need. Paying it forward not only strengthens your community but will reinforce the importance of support in your own life. This mutual support will not only bolster your emotional fortitude but will create a powerful network that extends beyond the confines of your job search, enriching both your professional and personal life.

Consider writing thank you notes to people who've helped you along the way. A simple gesture of gratitude goes a long way in strengthening these relationships. Schedule regular catchups, even if it's just for a quick phone call. These simple acts will not only show your appreciation but also help maintain a robust support network that can sustain you during future challenges. Your support network is not merely a temporary resource; it's an asset to be cultivated throughout your professional life, offering ongoing encouragement and perspective as your career continues to evolve. And that's a support system worth investing in.

Your therapist will not tell you to quit your job, but she'll guide you through what is possibly the best hard decision you can make.

8. You Should Just Give Up

Your therapist is not going to tell you to give up.... Ever.

When facing seemingly insurmountable obstacles and an uncertain future, resilience proves the ultimate determinant of success. It's not about avoiding hardship, but about masterfully maneuvering through it, deftly adapting to adversity, and uncovering inner strength in the crucible of challenge. Resilience acts as a robust mental buffer, absorbing life's jolting blows with grace and fortitude. Cultivate resilience as a critical resource. Like any powerful competency, it flourishes through consistent honing and diligent nurturing. It's not an innate talent reserved for a privileged few; instead, it's a pliable skill sharpened through determined effort. This involves cultivating a mindset that transforms difficulties, not into insurmountable roadblocks, but into rich soil for personal evolution and profound learning.

A fundamental element of resilience is unwavering optimism. Those with a resilient spirit view setbacks as transient hurdles, not permanent failures. They strategically focus on the positive, even in the darkest of times. They hold an unshakeable conviction in eventual progress, maintaining a hopeful outlook even when confronting daunting trials. This is not about ignoring stark realities; rather, it's about concentrating intently on achievable solutions and steadfastly believing in a positive resolution.

Consider the example of an entrepreneur whose startup fails. A person lacking resilience might dwell on the financial losses and personal setbacks, concluding that they're a failure and giving up on their entrepreneurial dreams. Someone with resilience, however, would analyze what went wrong, learn from their mistakes, and use this experience to inform their next venture. They'd view failure as a valuable learning experience, a steppingstone towards future success.

Another vital ingredient in the recipe for resilience is self-efficacy. Self-efficacy is the belief in your ability to succeed in a specific situation or accomplish a particular task. It's about having confidence in your skills and capabilities, even when facing uncertainty or adversity. People with high self-efficacy are more likely to persevere in the face of challenges, viewing obstacles as hurdles to overcome rather than insurmountable walls. They're more likely to set ambitious goals and persist in their efforts, even when setbacks occur.

Imagine a job applicant who receives multiple rejections. Someone with low self-efficacy might interpret these rejections as a sign of their inadequacy, concluding that they're simply not good enough for the jobs they're applying for. Someone with high self-efficacy, on the other hand, would analyze their application materials, refine their interview skills, and continue to apply for positions, viewing each rejection as an opportunity for improvement rather than a reflection of their inherent abilities. They understand that setbacks are a normal part of the job search process and maintain confidence in their eventual success.

Social support, as we discussed in the previous section, plays a pivotal role in fostering resilience. Having a strong network of friends, family, and colleagues who offer encouragement, empathy, and practical assistance can significantly enhance your ability to cope with stress and overcome challenges. Knowing that you're not alone in facing adversity can provide a sense of comfort and support, making it easier to persevere through difficult times.

Think about the power of a simple phone call from a friend during a particularly stressful week. Knowing that someone cares and is willing to listen can make a world of difference, offering emotional support and helping you maintain perspective. This supportive network acts as a buffer against stress, providing a sense of belonging and validation that strengthens your ability to navigate challenging situations.

But resilience isn't just about bouncing back; it's about adapting and growing in the face of adversity. It's about learning from your experiences, developing new skills, and finding new ways of coping with stress. It's about fostering a growth mindset, embracing challenges as opportunities for learning and development, and viewing setbacks as valuable lessons that can shape your future success.

Consider the example of someone who experiences a major life change, such as a job loss or a serious illness. A person lacking resilience might become overwhelmed by the situation, feeling helpless and hopeless. A resilient individual, on the other hand, would actively seek out resources and support, develop new coping mechanisms, and focus on adjusting to the changed circumstances. They might seek out new job opportunities, learn new skills, or develop strategies for managing their health. They view the situation as an opportunity for growth and personal development, utilizing the challenge to build their strength and resilience.

Different types of resilience exist, each reflecting a unique way of adapting to adversity. Some individuals demonstrate resilience through perseverance, consistently pushing forward despite setbacks. Others exhibit resilience through adaptability, skillfully adjusting their strategies and approaches to match the evolving circumstances. Still others find resilience through acceptance, acknowledging the challenges they face and finding ways to live peacefully with them. The key is to identify the type of resilience that best suits your personality and circumstances. Experiment with different strategies until you find the approach that works best for you.

Moreover, resilience isn't a static trait; it's a dynamic process that evolves over time. Your ability to cope with challenges may fluctuate depending on your circumstances, your emotional state, and the support systems available to you. What works for you in one situation might not work in another, so it's essential to develop a diverse repertoire of coping mechanisms to handle a variety of challenges.

Developing resilience requires conscious effort and practice. It's not something that magically appears overnight.

It requires cultivating positive self-talk, practicing mindfulness and self-care, setting realistic goals, and building a strong support network. It involves regularly challenging negative thoughts and replacing them with more positive and realistic ones. It's about nurturing self-compassion, treating yourself with kindness and understanding, especially during difficult times. It's about maintaining a healthy lifestyle through regular exercise, balanced nutrition, and sufficient sleep. All these elements contribute to your overall well-being and enhance your capacity for resilience.

Regular reflection on your strengths and accomplishments helps solidify your sense of self-efficacy. Make a conscious effort to acknowledge your successes, both big and small. This helps build confidence and belief in your ability to handle challenges. Celebrate your achievements and allow yourself to feel proud of the progress you've made. This positive reinforcement will enhance your belief in your capabilities and fuel your resilience.

Furthermore, developing a growth mindset is essential for building resilience.

Embrace challenges as opportunities for learning and growth. View setbacks not as failures but as valuable learning experiences that can inform your future actions. This mindset shift transforms obstacles into steppingstones, fueling your motivation and perseverance.

Finally, remember that building resilience is a journey, not a destination. It's an ongoing process of learning, adapting, and growing. There will be times when you feel overwhelmed, and setbacks will inevitably occur. But by cultivating the skills and strategies discussed here, you'll be better equipped to navigate life's challenges, bounce back from adversity, and emerge stronger than ever before. Remember, resilience isn't about avoiding difficulties; it's about developing the inner strength and adaptability to overcome them, to transform challenges into opportunities, and to ultimately flourish amidst life's storms. Embrace the journey, and you'll discover the remarkable power of resilience within yourself.

Developing Coping Mechanisms

So, we've laid the groundwork for understanding resilience – that incredible ability to bounce back from life's inevitable curveballs. We've talked about optimism, self-efficacy, and the power of a strong support system. But resilience isn't just a passive trait; it's an active skill set, a toolbox filled with coping mechanisms you can consciously develop and deploy when facing adversity. This is where the rubber meets the road, where the theory transforms into practical, everyday strategies.

Think of coping mechanisms as your personal resilience arsenal. They're the techniques and strategies you employ to manage stress, navigate challenging situations, and maintain emotional equilibrium. Just like a seasoned chef has a variety of tools in their kitchen, you need a diverse range of coping mechanisms to tackle the wide array of challenges life throws your way. There's no one-size-fits-all approach; what works wonders for one person might be completely ineffective for another. The key is experimentation, self-discovery, and finding the methods that resonate with you and bring you a sense of calm and control.

Let's delve into some proven coping strategies. We'll start with a cornerstone of modern stress management: **mindfulness.** Mindfulness isn't about escaping your problems; it's about engaging with them fully, but from a place of grounded awareness. It's about observing your thoughts and feelings without judgment, acknowledging them as fleeting mental events rather than absolute truths. Think of your mind as a rushing river; mindfulness is like stepping onto the bank and observing the current flow by, without getting swept away.

Practicing mindfulness can be as simple as focusing on your breath for a few minutes each day. Notice the sensation of the air entering and leaving your nostrils, the rise and fall of your chest. When your mind wanders – and it will – gently redirect your attention back to your breath. There are countless guided meditations available online or through apps, offering structured practices to cultivate mindfulness. Even a few minutes a day can make a significant difference in your ability to manage stress and react to challenging situations with greater composure.

Beyond formal meditation, mindfulness can be integrated into everyday life. While washing dishes, pay attention to the warmth of the water, the texture of the soap, and the feel of the plates in your hands. When walking, notice the sensation of your feet on the ground, the sights and sounds around you. By consciously engaging your senses, you ground yourself in the present moment, reducing the power of anxious thoughts about the future or regrets about the past.

Next, let's talk about **physical activity.** Exercise isn't just about physical health; it's a powerful tool for managing stress and improving mental well-being. Physical activity releases endorphins, those feel-good chemicals that have mood-boosting effects. Regular exercise can alleviate symptoms of anxiety and depression, enhance sleep quality, and improve overall cognitive function.

The type of exercise doesn't matter as much as the consistency. Whether it's a brisk walk, a yoga session, a swim, or a dance class, find an activity you enjoy and make it a regular part of your routine. Even short bursts of activity throughout the day can be beneficial. Think of taking the stairs instead of the elevator or going for a quick walk during your lunch break. The key is to find something that fits into your lifestyle and that you genuinely look forward to.

In addition to mindfulness and exercise, **creative expression** offers a potent avenue for coping with stress and processing emotions. Creative expression can take many forms, from painting and drawing to writing, music, dance, or even cooking. It's about finding a way to externalize your inner world, giving voice to your thoughts and feelings in a non-judgmental space.

If you're feeling overwhelmed, try journaling your thoughts and feelings. Don't worry about grammar or style; just let your thoughts flow onto the page. This can be a powerful way to process emotions and gain clarity on challenging situations. Or, if you're musically inclined, pick up an instrument and let your feelings pour out through music. The act of creating something, whether it's a painting, a poem, or a song, can be incredibly cathartic and restorative.

Beyond these core strategies, there's a whole world of other coping mechanisms to explore.

Spending time in nature has been shown to reduce stress hormones and improve mood. Even a short walk in a park can have a positive impact on your mental well-being.

Connecting with loved ones provides emotional support and a sense of belonging. Talking to a friend, family member, or therapist can help you process your emotions and gain a fresh perspective.

Humor is another powerful tool. Finding the humor in a difficult situation can help you maintain perspective and reduce stress. This doesn't mean making light of serious issues, but rather finding moments of levity amidst the challenges. Laughter truly is the best medicine.

Setting realistic goals and breaking down large tasks into smaller, more manageable steps can reduce feelings of overwhelm. Instead of feeling paralyzed by a daunting goal, focus on small, achievable steps that move you towards your ultimate objective.

And finally, don't underestimate the power of **self-compassion.** Treat yourself with the same kindness and understanding you would offer a friend facing a similar challenge. Acknowledge your struggles, validate your feelings, and forgive yourself for mistakes. Self-compassion is not about self-indulgence; it's about recognizing your inherent worth and treating yourself with the empathy and support you deserve. Developing effective coping mechanisms is a journey, not a destination. It requires self-reflection, experimentation, and a willingness to try new things. Keep a journal to track which strategies work best for you in different situations.

Don't be afraid to seek professional help if you're struggling to manage stress or develop healthy coping mechanisms. A therapist can provide guidance and support in identifying and developing strategies tailored to your individual needs.

Remember, building resilience is an ongoing process, a continuous refinement of your personal arsenal of coping skills. The more you practice, the stronger your resilience will become, enabling you to navigate life's challenges with greater grace, composure, and ultimately, joy. It's about equipping yourself not just to survive the storms, but to thrive in them.

Building Self Compassion

We've explored several crucial coping mechanisms for building resilience – mindfulness, exercise, creative expression, connecting with nature and loved ones, and even humor. But there's one more vital tool in your resilience arsenal that deserves special attention: self-compassion. Think of it as the ultimate buffer against the harsh self-criticism that can often accompany setbacks and struggles. Without self-compassion, even the most effective coping strategies can lose some of their power.

Self-compassion, in its simplest form, is treating yourself with the same kindness, concern, and understanding you'd offer a dear friend facing a similar challenge. It's about acknowledging your pain and struggles without judgment, offering yourself the same empathy and support you readily give to others. It's a radical act of self-acceptance, recognizing that imperfection is part of the human experience. Many of us are masters of self-criticism, a relentless inner voice that judges our every move, amplifies our flaws, and minimizes our successes. This inner critic can be particularly harsh during difficult times, leaving us feeling overwhelmed, inadequate, and even more vulnerable. Self-compassion directly counteracts this negativity, offering a balm to soothe the wounds of self-judgment.

Consider this scenario: You've been working tirelessly on a project, pouring your heart and soul into it. Despite your best efforts, the project doesn't meet expectations. The critical voice inside might start to berate you: "You're a failure," "You're not good enough," "Why couldn't you have done better?" This inner dialogue fuels feelings of shame, guilt, and self-doubt, hindering your ability to learn from the experience and move forward.

Now, imagine approaching this situation with self-compassion. Instead of harsh self-criticism, you acknowledge your effort and dedication. You recognize that setbacks are a normal part of life and don't define your worth. You might say to yourself, "This is difficult, but it's okay to make mistakes. I did my best, and I can learn from this experience." This compassionate self-talk helps you to process your emotions without succumbing to self-blame and despair. It allows you to focus on growth and improvement rather than dwelling on inadequacy.

Self-compassion isn't about self-indulgence or ignoring your shortcomings. It's not about avoiding responsibility or excusing poor behavior. It's about acknowledging your imperfections with kindness and understanding, learning from mistakes without letting them define you. It's about recognizing that everyone makes mistakes and faces challenges, and that your worth is not diminished by them. So, how do you cultivate self-compassion? It's a skill, like any other, that requires practice and conscious effort. Here are some practical techniques:

Mindful Self-Awareness: The first step is to become aware of your inner critic. Pay attention to your thoughts and feelings, particularly during challenging times. Notice the self-critical voice and its harsh judgments. Simply observing these thoughts without judgment is a powerful first step toward interrupting their negative impact.

Self-Kindness: When facing difficulties, talk to yourself as you would to a cherished friend. Offer words of comfort, encouragement, and understanding. Instead of berating yourself for a mistake, acknowledge your pain and offer yourself compassion.

For example, if you miss a deadline, instead of saying, "I'm so stupid," try, "This is tough, but I'll get through this. I can adjust my schedule and learn from this experience."

Common Humanity: Remember that you're not alone in your struggles. Everyone experiences setbacks, failures, and disappointments. Recognize that imperfection is a shared human experience, and that your struggles are not unique or shameful. This perspective helps to normalize your challenges and reduce feelings of isolation.

Mindfulness Meditation: Mindfulness practices are incredibly effective for cultivating self-compassion. By focusing on your breath and observing your thoughts and feelings without judgment, you create a space for self-acceptance and kindness. Many guided meditations specifically designed to cultivate self-compassion are readily available online and through meditation apps.

Self-Compassion Break: This is a quick exercise you can do whenever you're feeling overwhelmed or self-critical. It involves three steps:

- **Acknowledge your suffering:** Name the difficult emotion you're experiencing. For example, "I'm feeling overwhelmed and frustrated."
- **Offer self-kindness:** Treat yourself with compassion, as you would a dear friend. Say to yourself, "This is painful, but it's okay to feel this way. It's understandable given the circumstances."
- **Common humanity:** Remind yourself that suffering is a shared human experience. Say, "Many people experience this kind of pain. I'm not alone."

Journaling: Writing about your experiences, feelings, and self-talk can be a powerful way to identify and challenge self-critical thoughts. Journaling allows you to process your emotions in a safe and private space, creating a greater sense of self-awareness and understanding. This self-reflection can naturally foster self-compassion.

Positive Self-Talk: Actively counter self-critical thoughts with positive and supportive affirmations. Instead of focusing on your shortcomings, highlight your strengths and accomplishments. Remind yourself of your resilience, your ability to overcome challenges, and your inherent worth.

Acts of Self-Care: Self-compassion is also expressed through acts of self-care. Prioritize activities that nourish your mind, body, and spirit. This could involve spending time in nature, engaging in hobbies you enjoy, getting enough sleep, eating nutritious foods, and practicing relaxation techniques. These acts of self-care are tangible expressions of self-compassion.

The path to self-compassion is a journey, not a destination. It requires consistent effort, self-awareness, and a commitment to treating yourself with the same kindness and understanding you would extend to a loved one. Remember, being kind to yourself isn't selfish; it's essential for building resilience and navigating the inevitable challenges of life. It strengthens your ability to cope effectively with stress, bounce back from setbacks, and live a more fulfilling and meaningful life. As you practice these techniques, you'll gradually develop a stronger sense of self-acceptance, self-worth, and overall well-being, ultimately enhancing your capacity for resilience. And remember, practicing self-compassion is not just a nice-to-have; it's a crucial element in building a life characterized by strength, resilience, and joy. It's the cornerstone upon which true and lasting resilience is built. The more you practice self-compassion, the better equipped you'll be to navigate life's inevitable ups and downs, not just surviving, but truly thriving, even when the going gets tough. It's about cultivating an inner strength that emanates from a place of self-acceptance and kindness. This is the heart of resilience.

Cultivating Positive Relationships
We've established the crucial role of self-compassion in building resilience. But resilience isn't solely an internal affair; it

thrives on a strong network of supportive relationships. Think of your social connections as the scaffolding that holds up the structure of your well-being – the stronger the scaffolding, the more resilient the structure. This isn't about having a massive social circle; it's about cultivating a few deep, meaningful connections that provide consistent support and understanding.

Imagine a sturdy oak tree weathering a storm. Its deep roots, anchoring it firmly in the ground, represent your inner resilience, cultivated through self-compassion and other coping mechanisms we've discussed. But the tree also relies on the interconnectedness of its branches, its leaves reaching out to sunlight and air – these are your relationships. They offer a vital source of strength and sustenance, helping the tree, or in this case, you, withstand the harshest winds.

Building and nurturing strong relationships isn't always easy. It requires effort, vulnerability, and a willingness to invest time and energy. But the rewards are immense, providing a buffer against stress, a source of comfort during challenging times, and a sense of belonging that enriches life immeasurably.

One of the most effective ways to cultivate positive relationships is through **active listening**. This goes beyond simply hearing what someone is saying, it's about truly understanding their perspective, empathizing with their feelings, and showing genuine interest in their experiences. It means putting down your phone, making eye contact, and offering verbal and nonverbal cues that demonstrate your attentiveness. It means asking clarifying questions, reflecting back what you've heard to ensure understanding, and suspending judgment. Imagine a friend confiding in you about a difficult situation at work. Active listening isn't about offering immediate solutions; it's about creating a safe space where they feel heard and understood.

Another key ingredient in strong relationships is **empathy**. It's the ability to step into someone else's shoes, to see the world from their perspective, and to understand their feelings, even if you don't necessarily agree with them. Empathy allows you to connect with others on a deeper level, building trust and strengthening bonds.

Consider a time when a close friend shared a challenging experience. Your ability to empathize, to understand their feelings, even if you've never been in a similar situation, made all the difference in providing support. Furthermore, **open communication** is paramount. This isn't about avoiding difficult conversations; it's about navigating them constructively and honestly. It involves expressing your thoughts and feelings clearly and respectfully, even when discussing challenging topics. It means listening actively to the other person's perspective and working together to find solutions or compromises. Remember a time when open communication resolved a conflict, making the relationship stronger than before. This illustrates how honest communication, even about difficult matters, can strengthen your bonds.

Beyond communication, **mutual respect** is the bedrock of any healthy relationship. It involves valuing the other person's thoughts, feelings, and opinions, even when they differ from your own. It means treating them with kindness, courtesy, and consideration. It involves respecting their boundaries and acknowledging their individuality. Imagine a close relationship based on mutual respect; the understanding and trust created are the pillars of resilience.

Cultivating positive relationships also involves **giving and receiving support**. This is a two-way street. It means offering help and encouragement to others when they need it and being open to accepting and supporting yourself when you're struggling. It's about recognizing that vulnerability is a sign of strength, not weakness.

Consider a time you offered or received support – the reciprocal nature strengthens the bond and builds resilience. Moreover, **shared activities and experiences** create strong bonds. It's about finding common interests and engaging in activities that you both enjoy. This could be anything from attending concerts and sporting events to playing games, cooking together, or simply spending time in nature. Shared experiences create lasting memories and strengthen the emotional connection between people. Recall shared activities with close friends or family; these memories are the threads of resilience, offering comfort during difficult periods.

In addition to building positive relationships, recognizing the importance of seeking help when needed is vital. Resilience isn't about facing every challenge alone; it's about knowing when to ask for assistance. This could involve talking to a trusted friend or family member, seeking professional help from a therapist or counselor, or joining a support group. Think about times when you reached out for help – how did that experience contribute to your resilience? It's not a sign of weakness, but strength.

Don't underestimate the power of **shared laughter**. Humor can be a powerful tool for building resilience. Sharing jokes, watching funny movies, or simply enjoying a good laugh together can help to diffuse tension, reduce stress, and create a more positive emotional atmosphere. Consider the times shared laughter strengthened your bonds and created a sense of lightness.

It's also important to understand that relationships, like any aspect of life, require **maintenance and nurturing**. This isn't a one-time action, but an ongoing process. Regular check-ins, expressing appreciation, and making time for each other are essential for keeping relationships strong and supportive. It's a commitment to investing time and energy into the relationships that matter most. Just as you nurture your physical health, you must nurture your social well-being.

Sometimes, despite your best efforts, relationships may falter or end. It's important to accept that this is a part of life, and to navigate these experiences with self-compassion and understanding. It's okay to grieve the loss of a relationship, and to seek support during this challenging time. Remember that self-compassion isn't merely treating yourself kindly; it also involves accepting the natural ebb and flow of life, including the complexities of relationships.

Let's illustrate these points with some real-life examples. Perhaps you're facing a difficult work situation. Instead of bottling up your stress, actively reach out to a trusted colleague, family member, or friend. Share your concerns and allow them to offer support and perspective. Their empathy and understanding can provide a sense of relief and help you strategize solutions. Conversely, imagine offering a listening ear to a friend grappling with a personal challenge. Your active listening and unwavering support solidify your bond, strengthening your mutual resilience.

Consider another scenario: You're feeling overwhelmed by life's demands. Instead of isolating yourself, schedule time for activities you enjoy with loved ones. Shared laughter during a movie night, collaborative cooking, or a casual walk in nature can create a sense of connection and ease the burden you carry. This intentional connection directly fuels your resilience. Finally, remember that cultivating positive relationships isn't a race; it's a marathon. It's about consistently investing in these connections, nurturing them through thick and thin, and recognizing their profound impact on your overall well-being and resilience. It's about building a safety net, a supportive community, that provides a buffer against life's inevitable storms. The strength of these relationships significantly impacts your ability to navigate challenges and emerge stronger on the other side. Embrace the journey, celebrate the connections, and recognize the profound role they play in building a resilient and fulfilling life. This network of support is not just a helpful tool; it's a cornerstone of your ability to not just survive, but to thrive, even in the face of adversity. Invest in these relationships; they are truly invaluable.

Maintaining a Growth Mindset

We've explored the power of self-compassion and strong relationships in building resilience. Now, let's equip ourselves with another crucial tool: a growth mindset. This isn't just about positive thinking; it's a fundamental shift in how we perceive challenges and setbacks. A fixed mindset sees obstacles as insurmountable proof of limitations, leading to avoidance and discouragement. In contrast, a growth mindset views challenges as opportunities for learning and growth, fueling perseverance and resilience.

Imagine a sculptor working with clay. Someone with a fixed mindset might see a flawed piece and immediately discard it, convinced of their inability to create something beautiful. But a sculptor with a growth mindset would view the imperfections as a chance to refine their technique, to learn from the mistakes, and to ultimately create a masterpiece. This is the essence of a growth mindset – embracing imperfections as steppingstones to progress.

The beauty of a growth mindset lies in its ability to reframe failure. In a fixed mindset, failure is a judgment of worth, a confirmation of inadequacy. This leads to feelings of shame, self-doubt, and a reluctance to try again. But a growth mindset sees failure not as an indicator of inherent ability, but as valuable feedback, a crucial piece of information that guides future efforts.

Think about learning to ride a bicycle. Most of us fell countless times before mastering the skill. Those falls weren't failures; they were learning experiences. Each fall provided insights into balance, steering, and coordination. Had we adopted a fixed mindset after the first tumble, concluding we "weren't good at it," we'd never have learned to ride. Instead, we viewed the falls as data points, adjusting our approach and persevering until success. This perspective extends far beyond childhood skills. Consider a professional setback, like a missed promotion or a failed project. A fixed mindset might interpret this as evidence of incompetence, leading to self-criticism and career stagnation. But a growth mindset would see it as an opportunity for self-reflection, identifying areas for improvement and developing new skills. It's about analyzing what went wrong, not beating yourself up about it.

Developing a growth mindset necessitates a multifaceted approach. First, wholeheartedly embrace the learning journey itself. Prioritize diligent effort and incremental progress over solely achieving the destination. Acknowledge and celebrate each milestone achieved, no matter how seemingly insignificant, recognizing the inherent value of the journey toward mastery. Instead of fixating on shortcomings, reflect on the substantial growth attained. Consider learning a new language: each incremental achievement—from mastering new vocabulary to holding even imperfect conversations—represents significant progress.

Second, transform challenges into invaluable opportunities for development. Harness the power of positive self-dialogue. Instead of succumbing to catastrophic thinking ("This is insurmountable; I'll never succeed"), reframe setbacks as pivotal learning experiences ("This outcome wasn't ideal, but what crucial lessons can I extract? How can I refine my approach?"). This transformative shift redirects focus from self-criticism to proactive, solution-oriented thinking.

Next, actively solicit constructive feedback, viewing it as a catalyst for self-improvement. Don't shy away from criticism; embrace it as a guide toward growth. Seek input from trusted mentors, colleagues, or peers, leveraging their insights to pinpoint areas demanding further development. Cultivate receptiveness to diverse viewpoints, recognizing their essential contribution to personal evolution. Reflect on past instances where feedback significantly enhanced your trajectory. Fourth, cultivate an unshakeable belief in your capacity for continuous improvement. Concentrate on your potential for growth, rather than being confined by current limitations.

Remember that skills are not static; they are malleable, strengthened through focused effort and unwavering perseverance. This unwavering belief serves as the cornerstone of resilience, empowering you to confidently navigate adversity. Fifth, embrace the lifelong pursuit of knowledge. A growth mindset recognizes learning as an ongoing process, extending far beyond formal education. Actively seek novel challenges and experiences, embracing opportunities for both professional and personal advancement. This commitment to continuous learning fosters adaptability, bolstering resilience and resourcefulness in the face of life's ever-changing demands.

To illustrate, envision a student grappling with a particular subject. Rather than surrendering to frustration, they can adopt a growth mindset by focusing on dedicated effort, proactively seeking assistance from instructors or tutors, and celebrating even minor gains in comprehension. They would view academic hurdles as chances to learn and advance, thereby cultivating resilience in the face of setbacks. Consider an entrepreneur whose business venture initially fails. With a fixed mindset, they might view this as a personal failure, giving up on their dreams. However, a growth mindset would lead them to analyze the reasons for the failure, learn from their mistakes, and adapt their business strategy, eventually leading to success. Failure is merely a detour, not the end of the road.

Think of an athlete who suffers a serious injury. A fixed mindset might lead to feelings of hopelessness and abandonment of their athletic career. But a growth mindset allows them to focus on rehabilitation, adapt their training, and redefine their goals, demonstrating resilience in the face of adversity. Furthermore, consider an individual struggling with a personal relationship. A fixed mindset might blame the other person and give up on finding connection, while a growth mindset would encourage self-reflection, identifying patterns, seeking support and resources for communication and relationship building. This approach would foster personal growth and stronger future relationships.

The development of a growth mindset is an ongoing journey, not a destination. It requires conscious effort and practice. It's about constantly challenging your own thinking and beliefs, replacing self-limiting thoughts with empowering ones. This ongoing self-reflection and adaptation are vital to building and maintaining a growth mindset, improving your capacity for resilience in all areas of life. Remember, it's not about avoiding setbacks; it's about learning from them, growing from them, and emerging stronger than before. Embrace the process, and the rewards will be immeasurable.

Your therapist wants to assist you in this journey and will not tell you to just give up.

Self-Reflection and Self-Discovery

We've laid the groundwork for resilience by cultivating self-compassion and a growth mindset. Now, let's delve into the heart of the matter: understanding yourself. This isn't about navel-gazing; it's about equipping yourself with the knowledge and insight necessary to navigate life's inevitable challenges with grace and resilience. Self-reflection and self-discovery are the compass and map that guide you towards a more fulfilling and meaningful life. Think of it as an internal GPS for your wellbeing. The journey of self-discovery begins with a simple, yet profound question: "Who am I?" It sounds straightforward, but the answer is rarely simple. It's a question that requires deep introspection, honest self-assessment, and a willingness to confront both your strengths and your weaknesses. It's not a one-time answer; it's an ongoing process of exploration and refinement. Think of it like peeling an onion – each layer reveals a new aspect of yourself, leading to a deeper understanding of your inner landscape.

One effective technique for self-reflection is journaling. Grab a notebook, a pen, and carve out some quiet time. Don't worry about grammar or eloquence; just let your thoughts flow freely onto the page. Start by simply noting down your thoughts and feelings throughout the day. What triggered positive emotions? What brought on negative ones? What patterns do you notice? Journaling provides a safe space to explore your inner world without judgment.

Consider dedicating specific journal entries to exploring your values. What principles guide your decisions? What truly matters to you? Is it family, creativity, intellectual stimulation, helping others, or perhaps a combination of many things? Understanding your values helps clarify your priorities and makes it easier to make choices that align with your core beliefs. This alignment is fundamental to a sense of purpose and fulfillment. Imagine someone whose highest value is family yet constantly prioritizes work over family time. The dissonance between values and actions can lead to inner conflict and unhappiness. Identifying your values helps you prioritize accordingly.

Next, consider your strengths. What are you naturally good at? What talents do you possess? What activities make you feel energized and engaged? Don't underestimate the power of your strengths. These are your superpowers, the aspects of yourself that can help you overcome challenges and achieve your goals. It's easy to focus on our weaknesses, but focusing on your strengths creates a sense of capability and empowerment. Try making a list of your strengths and then brainstorm ways you could leverage those strengths to improve your wellbeing. A person who excels at communication, for example, can use this skill to build stronger relationships, advocate for themselves, and even find more fulfilling work.

Once you've explored your values and strengths, turn your attention to your goals. What do you aspire to achieve? These could be long-term goals, such as a career change or completing a degree, or short-term goals, like learning a new hobby or improving a specific skill. Setting clear goals provides direction and purpose, giving you something to strive for.

Remember to make your goals SMART: Specific, Measurable, Achievable, Relevant, and Time-bound.

Vague goals like "be happier" are far less effective than specific, actionable goals like "exercise three times a week for thirty minutes" or "spend quality time with family every Sunday."

Self-reflection isn't limited to journaling. You can also use guided meditations, mindfulness practices, and even conversations with trusted friends or family members to delve deeper into your inner world. Consider the use of prompts to stimulate self-reflection. Prompts can help us to think about specific aspects of our experience, and lead to more targeted reflection. For example: "Describe a time you felt truly alive," or "What is one thing you're grateful for today?"

Mindfulness exercises can be incredibly beneficial. Taking a few minutes each day to simply focus on your breath, noticing your thoughts and feelings without judgment, can lead to a deeper understanding of your emotional landscape. This increased awareness helps you to identify triggers, patterns, and emotional responses more effectively. This leads to a greater sense of control over your emotional wellbeing.

Another useful approach is to engage in activities that foster self-discovery. This could involve anything from trying new hobbies and exploring different interests to taking personality tests or attending workshops on personal development. These activities can help you uncover hidden talents, preferences, and passions that you may not have been aware of.

Remember that self-reflection is an ongoing process, not a one-time event. It's a journey of continuous learning and growth. There will be times when you feel lost or confused, and that's okay. The important thing is to keep exploring, keep questioning, and keep seeking a deeper understanding of yourself. Be patient with yourself; self-discovery takes time.

Let's explore some practical examples. Imagine Sarah, a high-achieving lawyer constantly feeling burnt out. Through journaling, she discovers that her core value is connection, yet her career demands constant isolation and competition. This insight leads her to explore alternative career paths that allow for more collaboration and human interaction. She utilizes her excellent communication skills, one of her identified strengths, to transition into mediation.

Or consider Mark, struggling with anxiety. He starts a mindfulness practice and, through self-reflection, identifies his anxiety triggers—perfectionism and a fear of failure. This awareness allows him to develop coping strategies, such as reframing negative thoughts and setting realistic expectations. He also identifies a strength – his creativity – and starts painting as a means of emotional regulation.

Self-reflection isn't about fixing what's "wrong" with you; it's about understanding yourself more completely. It's about embracing your imperfections, celebrating your strengths, and aligning your life with your values. It's about recognizing that growth and change are inherent parts of life, and that self-awareness is a powerful tool for navigating this ongoing process. By embracing self-reflection and self-discovery, you equip yourself not just with the resilience to overcome challenges, but also the wisdom to create a life that is genuinely fulfilling and meaningful. It's a journey of continuous exploration, revealing your true north and guiding you toward a more authentic and balanced life. The more you understand yourself, the better equipped you are to navigate the complexities of life and create lasting wellbeing. And isn't that worth the effort?

Setting Realistic Goals and Expectations
We've explored the power of self-discovery, unearthing your values, strengths, and aspirations. Now, let's translate that insightful self-awareness into actionable steps: setting realistic goals and expectations. This isn't about dampening your enthusiasm; it's about harnessing it effectively. Think of it like building a skyscraper: you can't simply erect the entire structure in a single day. You need a solid foundation, carefully constructed floors, and meticulous attention to detail. Similarly,

achieving significant personal growth requires a structured approach.

The most common pitfall in the pursuit of wellbeing is setting goals that are either too vague or too ambitious. "Become happier" is a noble aspiration, but it's as useful as a compass pointing in all directions at once. It lacks the specificity needed to guide your efforts. Instead, we need to break down large, overarching goals into smaller, bite-sized, achievable chunks. This approach prevents overwhelm, maintains momentum, and allows for consistent progress, which is crucial for sustaining motivation.

Let's use the example of someone aiming to improve their physical health. Instead of the sweeping goal of "get in shape," which is inherently subjective and difficult to measure, we can break this down into smaller, specific goals. This might involve setting a target of walking for 30 minutes three times a week, gradually increasing the duration and intensity over time. This approach offers a clearer path, a sense of accomplishment with each achieved step, and an opportunity to adjust the plan

based on progress and any
unexpected challenges that arise.
This principle of breaking down large goals
applies to all aspects of wellbeing:

Mental Wellbeing: If your goal is to reduce
stress, instead of aiming for immediate
stress-free existence (an unrealistic
expectation!), start with smaller, manageable
steps. This could include incorporating daily
meditation for 5 minutes, practicing deep
breathing exercises throughout the day, or
setting aside specific times for relaxation
and unwinding. Gradually increasing the
duration or frequency of these practices will
lead to a noticeable improvement in stress
management over time.

Emotional Wellbeing: If you're striving to
improve emotional regulation, begin by
identifying your triggers and developing
coping mechanisms for specific situations.
Perhaps you get easily frustrated in traffic. A
realistic goal might be to practice mindful
breathing or listen to calming music during
your commute for a week. The focus is not
on eliminating frustration entirely, but on

developing a manageable strategy to mitigate its impact.

Social Wellbeing: If you're aiming to build stronger relationships, start small. Instead of aiming to become incredibly popular overnight, focus on one or two meaningful connections. This could involve scheduling regular coffee dates with a friend, joining a social group aligned with your interests, or simply making a conscious effort to engage more deeply in existing relationships.

The SMART goal-setting framework provides a helpful structure:

Specific: Clearly define your goal. Avoid ambiguity. Instead of "eat healthier," aim for "eat at least five servings of fruits and vegetables daily."

Measurable: Track your progress. Use quantifiable metrics. Instead of "exercise more," aim for "exercise for 30 minutes, three times a week."

Achievable: Set realistic goals aligned with your capabilities. Don't set yourself up for failure by striving for the impossible. Start small and gradually increase the challenge.

Relevant: Ensure your goals align with your values and overall aspirations. A goal that feels irrelevant will quickly lose its appeal.

Time-bound: Set a deadline to maintain focus and motivation. Instead of "learn a new language," aim for "learn basic conversational phrases in Spanish within three months."

Let's look at some practical examples to further illustrate this point:

Imagine someone struggling with procrastination. Their overarching goal might be "become more productive." This is too broad. A more realistic and SMART approach would be: "Complete one specific task from my to-do list every morning before 10 AM for the next month." This breaks the goal down into manageable daily actions, making it less daunting and increasing the likelihood of success. The measurable aspect is the completion of the task, the achievable aspect lies in the manageable nature of one task per day, and the time-bound element is the daily before 10 AM and the monthly time frame.

Similarly, consider someone seeking to improve their sleep quality. Instead of vaguely aiming for "better sleep," a more effective goal would be: "Go to bed and wake up at the same time each day, including weekends, for four weeks, to regulate my sleep cycle." This goal is specific, measurable (tracking sleep times), achievable (relatively easy to implement), relevant to improved sleep quality, and time-bound (four weeks).

Setting realistic expectations also involves anticipating setbacks. Life throws curveballs. Unexpected events, personal challenges, or simply a lack of motivation can derail progress. This is completely normal. Don't beat yourself up if you miss a day of exercise, deviate from your diet, or postpone a task. Instead, acknowledge the setback, learn from it, and adjust your plan accordingly. The key is to maintain flexibility and avoid perfectionism, which can be a significant obstacle to progress. Self-compassion is your ally here –treat yourself with the same kindness and understanding you'd offer a friend facing similar challenges.

Remember, the journey to wellbeing is a marathon, not a sprint. Celebrate your successes, no matter how small, and learn from your setbacks. Consistent effort, combined with realistic goals and expectations, will lead to significant progress over time. And that's the beauty of it – the gradual accumulation of positive changes compounding to create a meaningful shift in your overall wellbeing. Be patient, be persistent, and celebrate the journey. You've already taken the most important step – recognizing the need for change and actively seeking a path to wellbeing. Now, let's continue to build that path, one solid step at a time.

Practicing Self Care and Mindfulness

Now that we've established a framework for setting realistic and achievable goals, let's delve into the crucial practices of self-care and mindfulness. These aren't mere luxuries; they're essential pillars supporting the structure of your wellbeing. Think of them as the regular maintenance checks on your metaphorical skyscraper –ensuring everything runs smoothly and preventing those pesky cracks from forming.

Self-care often gets misunderstood as frivolous indulgence – a bubble bath and a face mask once a month. While those things can be enjoyable and contribute to relaxation, true self-care is far more encompassing. It's about proactively tending to your physical, emotional, and mental needs, preventing burnout before it even sparks. It's about recognizing your individual needs and responding to them with intention and kindness. What constitutes self-care will vary wildly from person to person. For some, it's a quiet hour with a book, for others it's a high-energy Zumba class. The key is finding what genuinely nourishes *you*.

Let's explore some practical self-care strategies, categorized for clarity, but remember, these categories often overlap and intertwine:

Physical Self-Care: This is the foundation – the solid bedrock of your wellbeing. It encompasses the basics: sufficient sleep, regular exercise, and a balanced diet. We're not talking about extreme diets or grueling workout routines; think sustainable habits. Aim for 7-8 hours of quality sleep, incorporate at least 30 minutes of moderate-intensity exercise most days of the week – this could be a brisk walk, a bike ride, a dance class, or anything that gets your heart pumping – and prioritize nutrient-rich foods over processed junk. Listen to your body; it's a powerful indicator of your needs. Are you constantly craving sugary snacks? Perhaps you need more sleep or less stress. Are you feeling sluggish and fatigued? Maybe you need more movement or a nutrient boost. Pay attention to these signals and respond accordingly.

Beyond the basics, consider incorporating practices like regular check-ups with your doctor and dentist, ensuring you're up to date with vaccinations, and addressing any physical ailments promptly.

Physical self-care also extends to maintaining good hygiene, dressing in comfortable clothes, and ensuring your living space is clean and organized. A clutter-free environment can significantly reduce stress and improve your overall mood.

Emotional Self-Care: This involves cultivating emotional intelligence – understanding and managing your feelings effectively. This is where the work of setting realistic expectations and celebrating small victories truly shines. Emotional self-care isn't about suppressing negative emotions; it's about acknowledging them, processing them healthily, and developing coping mechanisms.

Journaling can be an incredibly powerful tool here. Simply writing down your thoughts and feelings can help you process them, identify patterns, and gain perspective. Talking to a trusted friend, family member, or therapist can also provide valuable support and guidance. Learning to identify and challenge negative self-talk is another key component. Replace those self-critical thoughts with kinder, more compassionate ones. Remember, you are worthy of self-compassion, even when you stumble.

Mental Self-Care: This focuses on maintaining a healthy mental state. Stress management is paramount. Incorporate mindfulness practices such as meditation, deep breathing exercises, or yoga into your routine. These techniques can help calm your nervous system, reduce anxiety, and improve focus. Even five minutes of daily meditation can make a significant difference. Engage in activities that stimulate your mind and bring you joy. This could be reading, learning a new skill, solving puzzles, playing a musical instrument, or pursuing any hobby that captures your interest. The key is to engage your brain in activities that are both challenging and enjoyable. Mental self-care also includes setting boundaries, saying no to commitments that overwhelm you, and prioritizing your mental health.

Social Self-Care: Humans are social creatures; our wellbeing is inextricably linked to our relationships. Nurturing meaningful connections is vital for mental and emotional health. Make time for friends and family, engage in activities you enjoy with others, and build a supportive network of people who understand and care about you. This could be joining a book club, volunteering for a cause you believe in, or simply scheduling regular coffee dates with loved ones. Don't underestimate the power of social connection. Feeling connected and supported can buffer against stress and promote resilience.

Spiritual Self-Care: This aspect focuses on connecting with something larger than yourself – whether it's a religious belief, nature, or a sense of purpose. Engaging in spiritual practices can provide a sense of meaning, purpose, and connection. This could involve prayer, meditation, spending time in nature, or engaging in acts of service. Connecting with your spiritual side can foster feelings of peace, contentment, and resilience.

Mindfulness In Self-Care:
Mindfulness, simply put, is the practice of paying attention to the present moment without judgment. It's about observing your thoughts, feelings, and sensations without

getting carried away by them. It's a powerful tool for managing stress, improving focus, and enhancing self-awareness.

There are many ways to incorporate mindfulness into your daily life. Mindful breathing is a simple yet effective technique. Focus on your breath as it enters and leaves your body, noticing the sensation of the air against your nostrils and the rise and fall of your chest. When your mind wanders – and it will – gently redirect your attention back to your breath.

Mindful walking is another great practice. Pay close attention to the sensation of your feet hitting the ground, the movement of your body, and the sights and sounds around you. Engage all your senses– notice the colors, textures, smells, and sounds of your environment.

Mindful eating is yet another powerful technique. Savor each bite, paying attention to the taste, texture, and smell of your food. Eat slowly and without distractions. Mindful eating can help you cultivate a healthier relationship with food and increase your awareness of your body's hunger and fullness cues.

Incorporating mindfulness into your daily routine doesn't require hours of dedicated practice. Even a few minutes each day can make a significant difference in your ability to manage stress and improve your overall wellbeing.

Integrating Self-Care and Mindfulness into Your Life:

The key to making self-care and mindfulness a sustainable part of your life is to start small and build gradually. Don't try to overhaul your entire routine overnight; instead, focus on incorporating one or two new practices each week. Find what resonates with you and adapt it to your lifestyle.

Experiment with different techniques until you discover what works best for you. Some people find meditation incredibly helpful, while others may prefer yoga or spending time in nature. There's no one-size-fits-all approach to self-care. The most important thing is to find practices that you enjoy and that support your overall wellbeing.

Schedule regular time for self-care and mindfulness practices. Treat these activities as non-negotiable appointments. Just as you wouldn't miss an important meeting, you shouldn't skip your self-care practices. Build them into your daily or weekly routine and make them a priority. Remember, self-care and mindfulness are not selfish; they're essential for maintaining your wellbeing and enhancing your ability to live a fulfilling life. By prioritizing your own wellbeing, you're better equipped to show up fully for the people and things that matter most to you. It's an investment in your present and future self, a promise to nurture the incredible human being you are. And that, my friend, is an investment worth making.

Seeking Professional Support When Needed

We've explored practical strategies for self-care and mindfulness, tools to build a stronger foundation for your wellbeing. But let's be honest, sometimes the cracks in our metaphorical skyscraper are a little too deep, a little too extensive for a DIY repair.

Sometimes, we need a more expert hand, a seasoned architect of mental wellbeing– a therapist or counselor.

Seeking professional support shows self-awareness, a recognition that you value your mental and emotional health enough to seek help when you need it. Think of it as proactive maintenance, not a crisis response. Just as you'd visit a doctor for a persistent physical ailment, seeking therapy for persistent emotional or mental challenges is equally vital.

Many people hesitate to seek therapy, often fueled by misconceptions. Some fear judgment, believing their problems are trivial or that they should be able to "handle it" on their own. Others are concerned about the stigma still associated with mental health treatment, a stigma that thankfully is gradually diminishing, but still lingers in some corners. And some simply don't know where to begin.

Let's address those concerns head-on. Your struggles are valid, whatever their size or nature. There is no such thing as a "too small" problem when it comes to your mental wellbeing. Therapy is a safe and confidential space to explore your challenges, without judgment or shame. Your therapist is there to support you, not to criticize you.

Finding the right therapist can feel overwhelming. It's a bit like finding the right pair of shoes – you need the right fit, the right style, and the right comfort level. Start by doing some research. Your primary care physician can often provide referrals, as can friends, family members, or support groups. Online directories, such as Psychology Today's therapist finder, can help you locate therapists in your area, often allowing you to filter by specialization, insurance coverage, and even therapy style.

The initial consultation is crucial. It's an opportunity to meet the therapist, discuss your concerns, and assess whether there's a good therapeutic fit. Don't hesitate to ask questions about their experience, approach, and fees. The therapeutic relationship is a partnership, and a good fit is essential for successful therapy. If you don't feel comfortable or connected with a therapist, it's perfectly acceptable – even advisable – to seek out someone else. Finding the right match may take some time, but the investment is worth it.

What can you expect in therapy? Each session is typically a structured conversation, focused on your goals and concerns. Your therapist will provide a safe, supportive environment for you to explore your thoughts and feelings. They may use various techniques to help you process your experiences, identify patterns, and develop coping mechanisms. Expect honesty, empathy, and a non-judgmental approach.

The benefits of therapy are far-reaching. It can help you manage anxiety, depression, trauma, relationship problems, grief, and a wide range of other challenges. It can equip you with tools to manage stress, improve communication skills, develop healthier relationships, and increase self-awareness. Therapy is a journey of self-discovery and personal growth, empowering you to live a more fulfilling and meaningful life.

Let me share a few real-world examples, not to highlight specifics, but to illustrate the diversity of situations where therapy can be profoundly beneficial. I've worked with individuals struggling with anxiety related to public speaking, learning effective coping mechanisms and ultimately delivering compelling presentations with newfound confidence. I've guided couples navigating difficult transitions, rebuilding communication and finding new ways to connect and support each other. I've supported individuals grappling with grief, finding healthy ways to process their loss and begin to rebuild their lives. And I've worked with people facing chronic illness, using therapy to develop strategies for managing the emotional and psychological challenges that often accompany physical ailments.

Each experience was unique, each path to wellbeing different, but a common thread weaved through them all: the power of professional support, of having a skilled guide to navigate the complexities of human emotion and experience. Remember, seeking help doesn't diminish your strength; it amplifies it. It's an act of self-compassion, a recognition that we all need support sometimes. The journey toward wellbeing isn't always a solo trek; sometimes, it's about accepting the help offered and allowing others to walk alongside us. So, if you're considering seeking professional support, know that you are not alone, and that reaching out is a brave and wise choice. The path to wellbeing may be challenging at times, but with the right guidance and support, you can discover strength, resilience, and a deeper understanding of yourself. And that, my friend, is a journey worth embarking on.

Consider this: your physical health is paramount. You wouldn't hesitate to see a doctor for a persistent cough or unexplained pain. Your mental and emotional health deserves the same level of care and attention. Ignoring persistent emotional distress or mental health challenges only allows them to fester, potentially escalating into more serious issues. Proactive care is preventative care, and therapy can be an incredibly valuable investment in your overall well-being.

Think of your mental health as a garden. Sometimes, it thrives, bursting with vibrant blooms. Other times, weeds choke the growth, stifling the beauty and vitality.

Therapy can be likened to a skilled gardener, providing the necessary tools, knowledge, and support to cultivate a flourishing mental landscape. They can help you identify and remove the weeds—negative thought patterns, unhealthy coping mechanisms, unresolved trauma—while nurturing healthy growth—self-compassion, resilience, and a strong sense of self.

The therapeutic process is a collaborative one. You are the active participant, setting the goals and direction of your journey. Your therapist acts as a guide, providing support, strategies, and a safe space for self-exploration. It's a partnership built on trust, mutual respect, and a shared commitment to your well-being.

Remember, the initial steps can feel daunting. It takes courage to acknowledge that you need support, to reach out and seek help. But with each step you take, you're investing in yourself, in your future happiness and well-being. The path to wellbeing is often paved with challenges, but with the right tools and support, the destination is well worth the journey. And remember, you're not alone in this;

countless others have traversed similar paths
and emerged stronger, healthier, and more
fulfilled. You, too, can achieve a richer,
more balanced life. The first step is often the
hardest, but it's a step towards a brighter
future. And that future, my friend, is well
within your reach.

Embracing the Journey to Wellbeing
Embracing the journey to wellbeing isn't a
sprint; it's a marathon, a winding path
through diverse landscapes of emotion and
experience. There will be sunny days filled
with breakthroughs and moments of
profound self-understanding, and there will
be cloudy days, perhaps even storms, where
challenges feel overwhelming. The key is
not to avoid the storms, but to learn to
navigate them, to find shelter when needed,
and to emerge stronger on the other side.

Patience is your most valuable
compass on this journey. It's easy to get
frustrated when progress feels slow, when
the changes you hope for don't materialize
overnight. Remember that lasting change
takes time, that building resilience is a
gradual process, and that setbacks are

inevitable. Don't let temporary disappointments derail your efforts. Instead, view them as opportunities for learning and growth, as steppingstones on your path toward wellbeing.

Let's say, for example, you're working on managing your anxiety through mindfulness techniques. You might find that in the beginning, your mind races even during meditation, that the quiet stillness feels elusive. You might feel tempted to give up, to conclude that mindfulness isn't working for you. But persistence is key. Each attempt, even if imperfect, strengthens the neural pathways associated with calmness and self-awareness. Celebrate the small moments of stillness, the brief pauses in the mental chatter, as evidence of progress, however incremental. It's like learning to play a musical instrument. You don't expect to become a virtuoso overnight; you practice consistently, gradually refining your skills. The same principle applies to building emotional resilience and wellbeing.

Self-compassion is another essential companion on your journey. Be kind to yourself, especially during difficult times.

Treat yourself with the same understanding and empathy you would offer a close friend facing similar challenges. Avoid self-criticism, the harsh inner voice that judges your perceived failures and shortcomings. Instead, focus on self-encouragement, reminding yourself of your strengths and accomplishments. Acknowledge your efforts, regardless of the outcome. Remember that progress, not perfection, is the goal.

Consider this scenario: you've set a goal to exercise regularly as part of your holistic wellbeing plan. One week, you stick to your routine flawlessly. Next, life gets in the way—a demanding work schedule, unexpected family obligations, a sudden illness. You miss a few workouts, and your inner critic might start berating you for your "failure." But instead of succumbing to self-criticism, practice self- compassion. Acknowledge the challenges you faced, affirm your intention to return to your exercise routine, and then gently ease back into it. Don't let a temporary setback derail your commitment to self-care. Self-compassion is about recognizing your humanity, acknowledging your imperfections, and treating yourself with kindness and understanding.

Celebrating small victories is crucial for maintaining motivation and momentum. Don't underestimate the power of acknowledging even the smallest achievements along the way. These small wins, often overlooked, serve as powerful reminders of your progress, reinforcing your belief in your ability to achieve your goals. They build confidence and foster a sense of accomplishment, motivating you to keep moving forward. Instead of focusing solely on the ultimate destination, take time to appreciate the milestones you reach along the way.

Think of completing a challenging jigsaw puzzle. You might feel overwhelmed by the sheer number of pieces initially. But as you start to assemble sections, you experience a sense of progress, a small victory each time a piece fits perfectly into place. This incremental success encourages you to continue, building momentum as you approach the final image. The same holds true for your journey to wellbeing. Celebrate those moments where you successfully manage stress, communicate assertively, or practice self-care effectively.

Let's illustrate this with another example. Suppose you're working on improving your communication skills, a critical aspect of healthy relationships. You might start by practicing active listening in a single conversation. This might involve paying close attention to the other person, asking clarifying questions, and reflecting back what you've heard to ensure understanding. This is a small victory, a step towards more effective communication. Acknowledge this accomplishment, no matter how seemingly insignificant. It builds confidence and motivates you to continue practicing your skills, aiming for increasingly complex interactions.

The journey to wellbeing is a process, not a destination.

It's a continuous cycle of self-discovery, growth, and adjustment. There will be times when you feel you're making significant strides, and there will be times when you experience setbacks. That's perfectly normal. The key is to maintain your commitment to self-care, to practice patience and self-compassion, and to celebrate your small victories along the way. Remember that every step you take, no matter how small, brings you closer to a richer, more fulfilling life.

Embrace the journey itself. It's in the process of navigating challenges, learning from setbacks, and celebrating small triumphs that you truly discover your strength, resilience, and the depth of your own capacity for growth. Don't be afraid to ask for support; remember that seeking guidance isn't a sign of weakness, but a testament to your commitment to your well-being. Surround yourself with supportive friends, family, and professionals who can offer encouragement and guidance.

Finally, remember that this is your journey, uniquely yours. There's no one-size-fits-all approach to wellbeing. Find what works best for you, and don't hesitate to adapt your strategies as needed. Be flexible, be patient, and be kind to yourself. The journey to wellbeing is a marathon, not a sprint, and you can reach your destination with dedication, self-compassion and the right support system. And let's face it, a little humor along the way never hurts either. After all, laughter is the best medicine, and a healthy dose of self-deprecating humor can be surprisingly therapeutic. So, embrace the journey, enjoy the process, and celebrate your amazing self along the way. You've got this!

Glossary

This glossary provides definitions of key terms used throughout the book. While the language is designed to be accessible, familiarizing yourself with these concepts may provide additional clarity.

Cognitive Behavioral Therapy (CBT): A type of therapy that helps individuals identify and change negative thinking patterns and behaviors.

Dialectical Behavior Therapy (DBT): A type of therapy that teaches coping skills to manage intense emotions and improve relationships.

Psychotherapy: A general term for treating mental health issues by talking to a therapist.

Psychodynamic Therapy: A type of therapy that explores unconscious patterns and past experiences to understand current issues.

Exposure Therapy: A technique used to treat anxiety disorders by gradually exposing individuals to feared situations or objects.

Stress-Related Terms

Stressors: Events or situations that cause stress.

Eustress: Positive stress that can be motivating.

Distress: Negative stress that can be harmful.

Stress Management: Techniques used to cope with stress, such as exercise, meditation, or relaxation techniques.

Coping Mechanisms: Strategies used to deal with stress and difficult situations.

Depression-Related Terms

Major Depressive Disorder (MDD): A severe form of depression characterized by persistent sadness, loss of interest, and other symptoms.

Persistent Depressive Disorder (PDD): A less severe but longer-lasting form of depression.

Postpartum Depression: Depression that occurs after childbirth.

Seasonal Affective Disorder (SAD): Depression that occurs during certain seasons, usually winter.

Anhedonia: Loss of interest or pleasure in activities.

Mental Health-Related Terms

Mental Wellness: A state of emotional, psychological, and social well-being.
Stigma: Negative attitudes and beliefs about mental illness.

Resilience: The ability to bounce back from adversity.

Self-Care: Practices that promote physical and mental well-being.

Mental Health Professional: A licensed professional who provides mental health services.

Author Biography

Carolyn Miller is a Licensed Clinical Social Worker and owner of The Healing Point, PLLC in Wilmington, North Carolina. After eighteen years as a practicing clinician, she has a knack for making complex psychological concepts both accessible and humorous, combining clinical expertise with a relatable writing style. Mrs. Miller is an entrepreneur and a lifelong student, seeking her next adventure around every corner. In her free time, Mrs. Miller enjoys coffee shops, reading, running, and traveling. She believes that laughter is the best medicine (and that a good cup of coffee can help solve almost any problem).

75437882R00179